That Takes the Cookie

That Takes the Cookie

85 Tasty Treats for Every Occasion

Ryan Alvarez and Adam Merrin
Creators of Husbands That Cook

SIMON
ELEMENT

NEW YORK | LONDON
TORONTO | SYDNEY
NEW DELHI

SIMON
ELEMENT

An Imprint of Simon & Schuster, LLC
1230 Avenue of the Americas
New York, NY 10020

First Simon Element hardcover edition November 2024

SIMON ELEMENT is a trademark of Simon & Schuster, LLC

Simon & Schuster: Celebrating 100 Years of Publishing in 2024

For information about special discounts for bulk purchases, please contact Simon
& Schuster Special Sales at 1-866-506-1949 or business@simonandschuster.com.

The Simon & Schuster Speakers Bureau can bring authors to your live event. For
more information or to book an event, contact the Simon & Schuster Speakers
Bureau at 1-866-248-3049 or visit our website at www.simonspeakers.com.

Photography by Lauren Volo
Interior design by Kristina Juodenas

Manufactured in China

1 3 5 7 9 10 8 6 4 2

Library of Congress Control Number: 2024937346

ISBN 978-1-6680-3293-0
ISBN 978-1-6680-3294-7 (ebook)

contents

3 Frosted and Filled

4 Cute and Colorful

5 Cookies 'Round the World

6 A Bar Walks into a Cookie...

7 Cookie Mash-Ups

introduction

Congratulations are in order— you just won the cookie lottery!

Whether you picked up this cookbook for yourself or you're looking for a gift for the home baker in your life, we're excited you're here. Before we get this baking extravaganza started, can we take a moment to acknowledge the awesomeness of cookies? Even the word cookie—derived from the Dutch *koekje*—is fun to say! It's no secret that everyone loves cookies. There's nothing better than a freshly baked cookie, hot out of the oven, especially when it's The Perfect Chocolate Chip Cookie (page 44).

Cookies make the world go 'round. They spread joy and happiness wherever they go. Think about it: How do you cheer up a friend having a rough day? Cookies. How can you get your kids to finally finish their chores? Cookies. What is guaranteed to make your sweetheart say yes to that romantic proposal? You guessed it: Sticky Toffee Pudding Cookies (page 234).

There's a cookie that's suitable for every occasion: birthdays, holidays, rainy days, sunny days, parties, date nights at home, baking projects with kids, and they make sweet gifts for your friends and family. We've included tasty treats for every situation like Peppermint Mocha Ice-Cream Sandwiches (page 100) to cool you off on hot summer afternoons, and easy, no-bake recipes like Quick Butterscotch Pralines (page 62) that will swiftly satisfy your midnight munchies. Our goal is to bring as many smiles, memorable moments, and profound *Mmmm*'s as we can to cookie lovers across the globe.

We had the best time creating the cookies in this book. Each one was made with lots of love and a little bit of sugar. You may be wondering if we have a favorite recipe. While we're asked this question frequently, it's nearly impossible to answer, as we love all our creations equally. But after careful cookie consideration, we decided that there is, indeed, one particular recipe in this book that takes the cookie for us. But, we wouldn't want to offend any of our beloved treats, so we'll leave that cookie conclusion up to you.

Oops, our oven timer just rang—we gotta go. We hope you enjoy baking (and tasting) these cookies as much as we did. If they bring a smile to your face and a celebration to your place, then our job is complete, and That Takes the Cookie.

Happy cookie-ing!
—Ryan and Adam

kitchen basics

Welcome to our kitchen. Grab a seat, take a cookie, and make yourself at home. Throughout these next few pages, we'll highlight the basics you'll need to prepare any cookie in this book. Our recipes use common, easy-to-find ingredients, so anyone can jump right in and start baking. You won't need every tool we're about to mention—these are just suggestions to help get you started. Got cookie questions? We've got cookie clarifications. After reading this chapter, you'll be cookie-confident and ready to bake anything. So preheat your oven, turn up the music, and let's make some cookies. On your mark, get set, dough!

general baking tips

Eggs and Butter

When preparing cookie dough, eggs and butter should always be at room temperature. If either is too cold, they won't blend properly with other ingredients, which could result in overly dense or chewy cookies. To bring cold eggs to room temperature, place them in a bowl of warm (not hot) water and let them rest for 10 to 15 minutes. The easiest method to bring cold butter to room temperature is to simply leave it on the counter in a covered container for a few hours or even overnight. If you need to start baking right away but your butter is too cold, we have a quick solution: place a piece of parchment paper on the counter, and cut the cold butter into small cubes, arranging them in a single layer on the parchment. Let the butter rest for 15 minutes, or until it's soft when pressed gently. If your kitchen is particularly chilly, the butter may need to rest for an additional 5 to 10 minutes.

Oven Temperature

If you don't own a portable oven thermometer, we highly recommend getting one today. It's the best way to get a true reading of your oven temperature, and is an inexpensive tool that will help produce consistent baking results. Unfortunately, most home ovens display inaccurate temperatures, regardless of brand or price point. They either run too hot, too cold, or incorrectly notify you that they're preheated, even when far from the desired temperature. We keep our portable thermometer in the oven at all times. Oven thermometers are available in grocery stores and online.

Using Parchment Paper

This nonstick, heat-resistant, food-safe paper makes baking a breeze. When you line your baking sheets with parchment paper, your cookies will never stick again. Anytime you're baking bar cookies or brownies, line the baking dish with parchment to effortlessly lift the bars out of the pan and cut them into squares. To line a baking dish with parchment, first lightly grease the bottom and sides of the dish with unsalted butter—this helps the paper stick to the pan. Then, cut a strip of parchment the same width as the bottom of the dish, and long enough to hang over the edges by an inch or two. Press it into the bottom and sides of the pan, allowing the excess paper to hang over the edge of the dish. This versatile paper is also microwave-safe and cannot be replaced with wax paper.

Baking with Multiple Pans

If you're baking more than one sheet of cookies at a time, there are a few things to keep in mind. Since the top and bottom areas of most ovens are excessively hot, be sure to arrange the oven racks as close to the center of the oven as possible. Also, swapping the positions of the two pans halfway through the baking time will ensure that the cookies bake evenly.

Gluten-Free Baking

When purchasing gluten-free flour blends, look for brands labeled as "cup for cup," as they tend to be more like all-purpose flour. There are many brands available, and they all produce slightly different results. The recipes in this book were tested using all-purpose flour, so substituting a gluten-free flour blend may change the texture and flavor of the cookies.

Digital Scales

The fastest, easiest, and most accurate way to measure ingredients is with a digital scale. A cup of flour can vary widely depending on how it's scooped, but when you weigh 120 grams of flour on a scale, the results are the same every time. To weigh your ingredients, simply place a mixing bowl on the scale, press tare to set it to zero, then slowly add one ingredient until the desired weight is reached. To add the next ingredient, press tare again to set the weight to zero, and repeat the process. Using a scale couldn't be easier, and since you won't need measuring cups, there will be fewer dishes to wash.

This chart shows weights of some common ingredients found in this book: ▶

Ingredient	Grams per 1 cup
All-Purpose Flour	120 g
Butter	226 g
Granulated Sugar	198 g
Powdered Sugar	113 g
Brown Sugar	213 g
Cocoa Powder	84 g
Graham Cracker Crumbs	104 g
Cornstarch	113 g
Chocolate Chips	170 g
Mini Chocolate Chips	180 g
Molasses	340 g
Corn Syrup	320 g
Honey	336 g
Rolled Oats	89 g
Peanut Butter	270 g
Pistachios	140 g
Hazelnuts	120 g
Pecans	113 g
Walnuts	113 g
Raisins	150 g

ingredients

Flour and Grains

All-Purpose Flour: While there are numerous kinds of flours available, we only use all-purpose flour for the recipes in this book. The most accurate way to measure flour is with a digital scale, but if you don't have one, you can measure it the following way: first, fluff the flour with a spoon to loosen any clumps. Then, holding a measuring cup above the container of flour, spoon the flour into the cup until it makes a heaping pile. Use the back of a knife to level the flour, allowing the excess to fall back into the container. When purchasing, look for unbleached flour, which is less processed and isn't treated with harsh chemicals. To store flour, keep it in a sealed, airtight container away from light and heat for maximum freshness. Note that flour should not be consumed raw, as it sometimes contains harmful bacteria, so eating cookie dough is potentially unsafe and not recommended.

Rolled Oats: Also known as old-fashioned rolled oats, these whole grains add a nutty flavor and chewy texture to cookies, like our Chewy Oatmeal Raisin Cookies (page 50) and Bourbon Peach Pie Bars (page 216). Be sure to use rolled oats, since quick oats become mushy when baked, and steel cut oats are too hard and crunchy.

Cornstarch: Cornstarch is used in baking to thicken custards and fruit fillings. When mixed into cookie dough, it loosens the flour, resulting in baked goods that are extra soft and tender, like classic Alfajores with Dulce de Leche (page 165) and our Crème Brûlée Cookies (page 256).

Leavening

Baking Soda and Baking Powder: Baking soda and baking powder are the most common types of leavening in cookie recipes. They work similarly, but they're made from slightly different ingredients. Baking soda is 100 percent sodium bicarbonate, an alkaline salt that creates carbon dioxide when mixed with acidic ingredients like lemon juice, yogurt, buttermilk, or cocoa. Baking powder also contains sodium bicarbonate, but it's combined with additional acidic salts, making it useful for recipes without acidic ingredients. Both leavening agents create tiny bubbles that inflate the dough, allowing it to rise and resulting in light, airy baked goods. For best results, look for aluminum-free baking powder, as aluminum can react negatively with some ingredients and cause discoloration, especially in recipes made with fresh fruit.

Cream of Tartar: Despite its misleading name, cream of tartar is actually a white powder unrelated to either cream or tartar sauce. It's a powdered form of tartaric acid that is naturally produced in wine barrels during grape fermentation. Cream of tartar functions in two ways, depending on the ingredients it's mixed with. When added to whipped egg whites, the acid binds to the proteins, making them more solid, resulting in perfectly crisp and crunchy meringues. It also functions as leavening in doughs, which helps create extra-soft cookies like Mexican Hot Chocolate Snickerdoodles (page 240).

Active Dry Yeast: Active dry yeast is an essential ingredient in bread baking, which provides lift to doughs, causing them to rise. It is rarely used in cookie recipes, but it does make one appearance in this book. We use it to create a traditional yeasted dough in our Maple-Butter Belgian Waffle Cookies (page 251), which taste just like classic Belgian waffles. Active dry yeast is commonly sold in small packets for easy measuring.

Salts

Table Salt: All the recipes in this book use non-iodized table salt. Since other types of salt can have slightly different flavors and sodium levels, table salt provides the most consistent results.

Flaky Sea Salt: Flaky sea salt comes from evaporated seawater and is named for its rough, flaky crystals. It has a crunchier texture than table salt and a delicate flavor from the ocean minerals. It is always used as a garnish and is delicious when paired with dark chocolate, like in our Legit Toasted Almond Chocolate Chunk Cookies (page 72).

Dairy

Unsalted Butter: We only use unsalted butter in this book—never salted. Since salted butter contains various amounts of salt depending on the brand, using unsalted butter will produce the most consistent results. If you only have salted butter, reduce the salt in the recipe by ⅛ to ¼ teaspoon for each stick of butter used.

Heavy Cream: There are several kinds of cream available, but heavy cream provides the best results. Since it's higher in fat than regular whipping cream, it has a richer flavor and a thicker texture.

Milk: In this book, all milks are welcome! Anytime a recipe calls for milk, feel free to use the milk of your choice. Whether you decide to use low-fat, whole, or skim—or an alternative milk like oat, almond, or soy—any kind will work equally well.

Cream Cheese: Cream cheese should always be used at room temperature, since cold cream cheese doesn't blend well with other ingredients. For the best baking results, purchase full-fat cream cheese sold in blocks. Avoid whipped cream cheese sold in tubs, as it contains stabilizers and other additives, making it unsuitable for baking.

Buttermilk: Despite its name, buttermilk doesn't contain any butter. It's a low-fat, fermented dairy product that resembles a thin, pourable yogurt. Buttermilk contains live cultures and adds a tangy flavor to baked goods. If you don't have buttermilk, you can quickly and easily make a substitute: to make 1 cup of buttermilk, combine 1 cup milk of your choice with 1 tablespoon white vinegar or lemon juice, stir to combine, and let rest for 5 minutes.

Oils

Extra-Virgin Olive Oil: In this cookbook, extra-virgin olive oil is featured in a few recipes. It replaces butter and adds a light, peppery flavor to cookies like Lemon Olive Oil Pignoli (page 152) and Melomakarona Spiced Honey Cookies (page 159). To keep your olive oil fresh, look for brands with dark-colored bottles, and store them in a cool, dark place. Keep olive oil far from the stove, as it will spoil quickly when exposed to light and heat.

Vegetable Oil: Vegetable oil is used only once in this book. It has a neutral flavor and adds an extra-soft texture to our Crème Brûlée Cookies (page 256). When purchasing vegetable oil, look for neutral unflavored varieties like canola, soybean, or corn oil.

Sugars

Granulated Sugar: The recipes in this book wouldn't be the same without this sacred substance. Also known as white sugar, this sweet and versatile ingredient creates magic in nearly every cookie recipe. When melted on the stove, it turns into a golden amber syrup, which gloriously transforms into a rich, chewy caramel by simply adding a little butter, cream, vanilla, and salt. Wow your friends with Brown Butter Pecan Cookies with Salted Caramel Filling (page 84), drizzle it over our Sticky Toffee Pudding Cookies (page 234), or simply eat it by the spoonful.

Brown Sugar: Brown sugar contains natural molasses, which brings a toffee-like flavor and distinct dark color. While there are several varieties of brown sugar available, any kind will work with the recipes in this book. When measuring, use a scale for the most accurate results. If you don't have a scale, scoop the brown sugar into a dry measuring cup and press it in firmly with the back of a spoon until the cup is packed tightly. This eliminates air pockets, ensuring consistent results every time.

Powdered Sugar: Also known as confectioners' sugar, this finely ground powder is used to make smooth frostings and glazes.

It contains a small amount of cornstarch, which helps make cookies extra soft, like in our Iced Horchata Latte Cookies (page 92) and Luck of the Irish Cream Cookies (page 124). The most accurate way to measure powdered sugar is with a digital scale, but if you don't have one, you can measure it the following way: first, fluff the powdered sugar with a spoon to loosen any clumps. Then, holding a measuring cup above the container of powdered sugar, spoon the sugar into the cup until it makes a heaping pile. Use the back of a knife to level the sugar, allowing the excess to fall back into the container. Then sift the powdered sugar through a fine-mesh strainer to prevent clumping.

Maple Syrup: Maple syrup is a wonderful all-natural sweetener produced from the sap of maple trees. It's available in several grades of color; note that the darker the syrup, the more intense the maple flavor. Feel free to use your favorite kind, as any grade of maple syrup will work with these recipes.

Light Corn Syrup: Light corn syrup is a clear liquid sugar made from the starch of corn. It's used as a sweetener and thickening agent and is lightly flavored with vanilla and salt. It produces soft textures in recipes like homemade marshmallows (page 139) and melt-in-your-mouth marzipan (page 87). Since dark corn syrup has a significantly different flavor, it is not used in this book, and is not interchangeable with light corn syrup.

Honey: Thanks to honeybees, humans have been enjoying this all-natural, golden sweetener for over eight thousand years. With a similar sweetness to granulated sugar, each variety of honey is uniquely flavored depending on where it's produced. It is featured in two recipes in this book: Vanilla-Glazed Pfeffernüsse (page 168) and Melomakarona Spiced Honey Cookies (page 159). To keep honey fresh, store it in a cool, dark place. It is normal for honey to crystallize over time, so if this happens, place the container of honey in a bowl of warm water for 15 minutes to soften and dissolve the crystals.

Molasses: This thick, dark syrup is a liquid sugar made from sugarcane. Not only is it the source of most distilled rum, but it is also the main ingredient used to produce commercial brown sugar. Molasses is faintly sweet with a bitter earthiness and enhances gingerbread with its characteristic warm flavor. Do not substitute light molasses, which is more similar in flavor to maple syrup.

Eggs

Eggs are sold in different sizes, so use standard large eggs for the most consistent results. When purchasing, look for pasture-raised eggs with deep-orange yolks, as they are more flavorful than factory eggs. When cracking an egg, first break the egg into a small dish before adding it to the mixing bowl of other ingredients. This prevents any eggshell fragments from falling into the dough, and it allows you to inspect the egg for freshness first. To separate an egg using your hands, first cup your hand over a small bowl, then crack the egg into your hand. Separate your fingers slightly, allowing the egg white to drain into the bowl, while keeping the yolk between your fingers. Be careful not to break the yolk, because if it drips into the bowl, the egg whites will not whip properly.

Nuts

Whole Nuts: There are eight different types of nuts found in this book—almonds, peanuts, walnuts, pecans, hazelnuts, pine nuts, pistachios, and macadamia nuts—and each one brings a unique flavor and texture. Since nuts can become stale quickly, especially after being chopped, be sure to always use fresh whole raw nuts. For the most consistent baking results, purchase unsalted nuts, as each brand has varied salt amounts. The one exception is our Haunted Halloween Haystacks (page 138), which call for salted peanuts.

Almond Flour: This gluten-free flour is made from finely ground almonds. Its mild, nutty flavor is highlighted in several cookies throughout this book, like our Lemon Tart Linzer Cookies (page 103) and Raspberry-Filled Spitzbuebe Hearts (page 184). With a higher fat content than all-purpose flour, it brings additional moisture and a tender crumb to baking recipes. Almond flour is also the primary ingredient in marzipan, and our delicious homemade recipe is featured in Citrus Shortbread Cookies with Marzipan Filling (page 87) and Glazed Stollen Cookies with Marzipan (page 248).

Peanut Butter: When buying peanut butter for baking, look for brands that are creamy and don't require stirring. Avoid natural peanut butters, since their oils can cause baked goods to become greasy.

Extracts and Flavors

Vanilla Extract: This aromatic flavoring is an essential ingredient and appears in almost every great dessert. It can be expensive to purchase, but thankfully it's easy to make at home. Slice eight to ten whole vanilla beans in half lengthwise, then drop them into an empty 16-ounce glass bottle with an airtight cap. Fill the bottle with bourbon or vodka, then close the cap and shake gently. Label the bottle with the current date, and set it in a cool, dark place, shaking it every few weeks for six months to one year. At that point your patience will be rewarded—the flavor and color will have deepened, and you can begin to use your homemade vanilla extract in any recipe. After every use, top off the bottle with additional bourbon or vodka and shake gently. Also, any-time you're baking with whole vanilla beans, like Vanilla Bean Sugar Cookies (page 43), don't discard the beans. Instead, add the empty bean to your bottle of homemade vanilla extract! Using this method will give you an endless supply of vanilla extract, and you'll always be ready to bake a batch of cookies. When purchasing vanilla beans, it's most cost-effective to purchase them in bulk online, as the prices are much cheaper than in stores.

Coffee: The secret to bringing coffee flavor to baked goods without adding extra liquid is to use instant coffee crystals or instant espresso powder. Both products are similar, and can be substituted interchangeably in equal parts, if needed.

Spices: Spices are best when used fresh. Since their fragrance and flavor diminish with time, always check your spices for freshness before baking. Purchase spices in small containers, and store them in a cool, dark place away from heat.

Chocolate

Unsweetened Chocolate: Unsweetened chocolate doesn't contain any sugar and is 99% to 100% cacao. The flavor is extremely bitter, but when combined with sugar and other ingredients, it adds a rich, dark chocolate flavor to recipes like Chocolate Rainbow Meltaways (page 134).

Cocoa Powder: Unsweetened cocoa powder is 100% cacao with no added ingredients. It is available in two common types: natural cocoa and Dutch-process cocoa. Natural cocoa is reddish-brown, similar to devil's food cake, while Dutch-process cocoa is almost black, like Oreo cookies. Even though they have slightly different flavors, either kind will work with the recipes in this book.

Bittersweet Chocolate: The term "bittersweet" refers to chocolate that contains 60% to 75% cacao. The higher the percentage, the darker the chocolate will be. All the recipes in this book were tested with 65% bittersweet chocolate, but feel free to use the bittersweet chocolate of your choice.

Semisweet Chocolate: Semisweet chocolate contains approximately 45% cacao along with sugar and vanilla. It appears three different ways in this book: as chocolate chips, mini chips, and chopped bars of chocolate. Semisweet chips are featured in classic treats like The Perfect Chocolate Chip Cookie (page 44), while mini chips are used as a traditional—and tasty—garnish for Cannoli Cookie Cups (page 242). Recipes like Legit Toasted Almond Chocolate Chunk Cookies (page 72) call for chopped semisweet bars, resulting in pools of melted chocolate in every bite. While they all taste similar, each one provides a distinct texture.

Milk Chocolate: Milk chocolate contains approximately 25% to 30% cacao. While this type of chocolate isn't found in many cookie recipes, it is featured in our Toasted Marshmallow S'mores Cookies (page 264), inspired by classic campfire s'mores.

White Chocolate: White chocolate doesn't contain any cacao and is traditionally made with milk, sugar, and cocoa butter. It is featured in our Cranberry-Orange White Chocolate Chip Cookies (page 56) and melts into spooky Haunted Halloween Haystacks (page 138).

Color and Decorations

Food Coloring: Food coloring is available in only a few primary colors in most grocery stores, but hundreds of colors can be found in craft supply stores and online. For the most vibrant colors, look for gel food coloring, which is slightly thicker and richer in color than traditional liquid food coloring. The thicker texture of gel color allows it to be painted with a brush, creating pretty streaks of color, like in Citrus Meringue Drops (page 122).

Candy Melts: Also known as white chocolate melts, these colored candies don't contain any chocolate. They're sold in a rainbow

of colors and are designed specifically to melt evenly and create smooth coatings like in Strawberry Shortcake Marshmallow Cookies (page 139) and Toffee Crunch Cookie Dough Pops (page 126). Candy melts are available in craft supply stores and online.

Sparkling Sugar: This decorative sugar has large, glittering crystals. It reflects light and is the perfect garnish to add shimmer and crunch to holiday cookies and treats like Sparkling Party Pinwheels (page 145). Sparkling sugar is available in a variety of colors, like the shamrock green featured in our Luck of the Irish Cream Cookies (page 124).

Rainbow Sprinkles: The two most common types of rainbow sprinkles are jimmies and nonpareils. Jimmies are small, soft cylinders commonly used as an ice-cream topping, and non-pareils are tiny crunchy spheres. In recipes that call for rainbow sprinkles, like Colorful Confetti Sugar Cookies (page 120), either variety will work.

Fruits and Vegetables

Citrus: Fresh lemons, limes, and oranges are featured generously throughout this book. Anytime a recipe calls for citrus, always try to use fresh fruit. Since commercial bottled juices contain preservatives and additives that diminish the flavor, these products are not recommended. Whenever a recipe calls for grated zest and freshly squeezed juice, be sure to zest the fruit before juicing.

Jam: People often wonder what the difference is between jelly, jam, and preserves. Jelly is made with filtered fruit juice and doesn't contain any fruit chunks. Jam is made with fruit that's been crushed or mashed. Preserves contain whole pieces of fruit. The recipes in this book only call for jam, since jelly is too runny, and preserves are too chunky.

Sweetened Shredded Coconut: The most common kind of shredded coconut used for baking is the sweetened variety. Other kinds of coconut are dry and crisp with no sugar, so be sure to purchase the sweetened variety for the recipes in this book. It adds a tropical flavor to cookies like Macadamia-Coconut Shortbread with Passionfruit Glaze (page 177) and is featured in our Pumpkin Spice 7-Layer Bars (page 224).

Peaches: Fresh peaches are most flavorful in the summertime, but when they're not available, canned peaches work just as well.

When using canned peaches, be sure to buy fruit with 100% juice, rather than syrup, and drain the peaches thoroughly before use. When using fresh peaches, they will peel easily with the following method: bring a medium pot of water to a boil, place the peaches in the boiling water and cook for 30 seconds, then immediately transfer the fruit to a bowl of ice water and let rest for 1 minute. Remove the peaches from the ice water, then slide the skins off.

Apples: Anytime a recipe in this book calls for apples, we recommend Granny Smiths. Also known as sour apples, this green variety of the apple family is a popular choice for desserts, since their tart flavor mixes well with ingredients like brown sugar and cinnamon. Other apple varieties can become too soft when baked, but Granny Smiths have a crisp texture and hold their shape well. If Granny Smith apples are unavailable, any tart variety will work, such as Honeycrisp or Fuji. Apples should always be peeled before use, as the skin is tough and chewy.

Bananas: When selecting bananas for recipes like Chocolate Chunk Banana Bread Bars with Toasted Walnuts (page 205), look for ripe fruit that is yellow with a few brown freckles, but not covered in dark brown patches. Bananas that appear too brown are past their prime and the flavor may be degraded. Since banana slices can turn brown quickly when used as a garnish, cut them immediately before serving.

Raisins: Be sure to use newly purchased raisins when baking. The difference in flavor and texture between a fresh, soft, and plump raisin and an old, dried-out raisin is immense. To maintain optimum freshness, keep raisins sealed in an airtight container in a cool, dark place.

Freeze-Dried Berries: Freeze-dried fruits are versatile for baking and widely available in grocery stores. When ground into powder, they blend with flour to make intensely fruit-flavored cookies, like the raspberry shortbread in Peach Melba Shortbread Stacks (page 94). Powdered freeze-dried berries can also be used for flavorful and colorful glazes, like the pretty pink coating on our Strawberry Shortcake Marshmallow Cookies (page 139). When preparing the dried fruit powder, strain it through a fine-mesh strainer to remove any seeds for best results.

Alcohol

Rum: In this book, anytime a recipe calls for rum, like No-Bake Tropical Rum Balls (page 74), either silver rum or gold rum will work equally well. Since only a small amount is used in these recipes, the type of rum you choose will not make a significant difference.

Bourbon or Whiskey: Whenever a recipe calls for bourbon or whiskey, like Bourbon Peach Pie Bars (page 216), feel free to choose any kind of bourbon, rye, or other American-style whiskey. Do not use peaty Scotch whisky, as the intense smoky flavor will overwhelm the other ingredients . . . but feel free to sip some while you bake a batch of cookies.

Other

Graham Crackers: Graham crackers are used throughout this book, usually in the form of finely ground crumbs. Although packaged graham cracker crumbs are available in stores, it is recommended to buy whole crackers and grind them at home, since it is fresher and more flavorful. The quickest method to make graham cracker crumbs is with a food processor, but if you don't have one, simply place the graham cracker sheets in a zip-top bag and crush them with a rolling pin. It takes approximately six to seven graham cracker sheets to make 1 cup crumbs.

Marshmallow Crème: Also known as marshmallow fluff, this sticky-sweet confection is sold in the baking aisle of most grocery stores. It is whipped into fluffy fillings like in Gingerbread Whoopie Pies with Vanilla Marshmallow Crème (page 106), it's a traditional ingredient in homemade fudge, and it makes our Peanut Butter Pretzel Fudge Bars (page 210) extra chewy and delicious.

Marshmallows: For most cookie recipes, using mini marshmallows is ideal, since standard marshmallows are too large and can cause cookies to fall apart during baking. If mini marshmallows aren't available, simply cut standard-size marshmallows into ½-inch pieces.

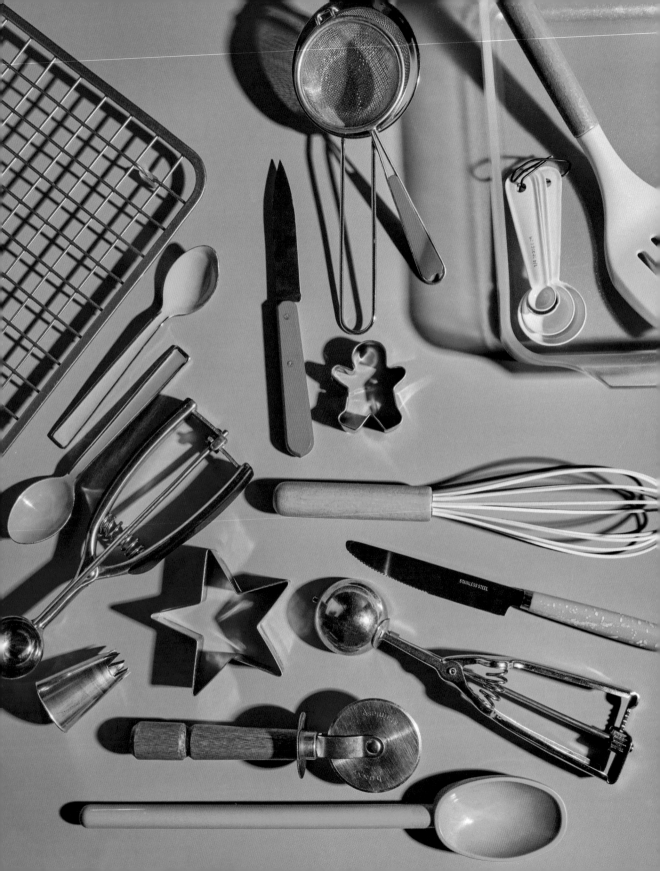

equipment

Electric Tools

Electric Mixer: Electric mixers are a baker's best friend. Most cookie recipes begin with beating butter and sugar, and electric mixers make the process quick and easy. The two most common types are stand mixers and handheld mixers. Stand mixers are more powerful than handheld mixers, and they allow you to work hands-free, since you can turn them on and prepare something else while they mix. Handheld mixers aren't as powerful, but they perform equally well, take up less space, and are often cheaper to purchase. When using either type, be sure to frequently stop the mixer and scrape the sides of the mixing bowl. If you don't own an electric mixer, you can stir any recipe in this book by hand instead.

Food Processor: Food processors are useful tools for crushing ingredients into powder. If one isn't available, use a large, sharp knife instead, which can achieve the same results, but will take more time.

Blender: Blenders are helpful tools for blending liquid ingredients. In this book, blenders are used to create everything from fruit purees—like the creamy peach curd filling in Peach Melba Shortbread Stacks (page 94)—to homemade ice cream for Peppermint Mocha Ice-Cream Sandwiches (page 100). Any kind of blender will work, but high-powered blenders produce noticeably smoother results. If a blender isn't available, a food processor can be used instead. If neither is available, you can puree ingredients using a potato masher or a sturdy whisk, but the results will not be as smooth.

Hand Tools

Silicone Spatula: Flexible silicone spatulas are used for a multitude of applications. They're ideal for stirring, as the thin blade can perfectly scrape the sides of mixing bowls. Also, they are heatproof up to 500°F (260°C) and can safely be used to stir simmering mixtures on the stove.

Offset Spatula: These small, thin tools are essential when decorating cookies. They have a dull metal blade bent at a slight angle, which helps frost desserts easily without your hands getting in the way. They're also useful for spreading batter evenly into baking pans—especially in hard-to-reach corners.

Wide Spatula: The easiest way to transfer warm cookies to a cooling rack is with a wide, flat spatula—the same tool used to flip pancakes. They're also occasionally used to flatten puffy cookies after baking. Be sure to use plastic or wood spatulas, as metal can scratch your cookware.

Whisk: Whisks are valuable kitchen tools for mixing ingredients. They combine dry ingredients evenly and will whip liquid ingredients when an electric mixer isn't available. While there are many sizes and shapes of whisks, the two most useful types are balloon whisks and French whisks. Balloon whisks have a wide, rounded shape made for stirring ingredients in large mixing bowls, and French whisks are narrower, which is helpful when whisking ingredients in small saucepans. If a whisk isn't available, using a fork can achieve similar results.

Wire-Mesh Strainer: This versatile tool is useful for sifting dry ingredients and straining liquids. It has a finely woven steel mesh screen made to catch the smallest ingredients. Wire mesh strainers remove lumps when sifting powders like flour and cocoa, and help produce perfectly smooth custards and fruit curds. When purchasing, select a strainer with tight mesh, as those with larger holes can allow pulp or seeds to pass through. Also, be sure that the strainer has hooks around the edges, which allow it to rest on top of a mixing bowl for easy sifting.

Rolling Pin: Rolling pins are indispensable kitchen utensils that help produce perfectly flat cookies and clean cutout shapes. They're available in a variety of styles and materials, from classic wooden pins to stainless steel, silicone, and marble—and they all work equally well. If no rolling pin is available, replace it with a heavy object of similar size, such as a wine bottle.

Silicone Rolling Mat: Silicone mats are useful when rolling out dough. They're made from a smooth silicone material, so dough won't stick. Also, they make cleanup a breeze, since the flour-covered mat can be gathered and brought to the sink, leaving a spotless countertop. When purchasing, look for silicone mats with measured grid lines and clearly marked circles, which allow you to easily see the dimensions of your dough while you roll it out.

Knives: Knives are available in many different shapes and sizes, but you will only need three types to prepare all the recipes in this book. The first is a large chef's knife, useful for chopping bars of chocolate, mounds of toasted nuts, and fresh herbs. Second is a small paring knife, ideal for slicing fruit and berries and making delicate cuts. Third is a large, serrated knife for cutting bar cookies into even squares. To maintain knives' sharpness, always hand-wash, as dishwashers can cause knives to dull quickly.

Cookie Dough Scoop: These handy scoops create equally sized balls of cookie dough every time. They're shaped like miniature ice-cream scoops and are commonly available in three sizes—1 tablespoon, 1½ tablespoons, and 2 tablespoons—all of which are used throughout this book.

Pastry Wheel Cutter/Pizza Cutter: Pastry wheel cutters and pizza cutters have round, rolling blades, which are useful for making long, straight cuts in dough, like in our Apricot-Pear Rugelach (page 174). If a cutter isn't available, a long chef's knife will work just as well.

Microplane Zester: Microplane zesters are the best tool for grating fresh citrus zest. They produce delicate, thin threads of zest, perfect for mixing into doughs and fillings. These versatile kitchen utensils are also used to finely grate spices like fresh nutmeg.

Citrus Squeezer: While there are many types of juicers available, handheld citrus squeezers are ideal for the recipes in this book. This inexpensive kitchen tool easily juices citrus with just one squeeze, while filtering out the seeds. Also, their one-piece, compact design means fewer dishes to wash than the multiple components of large electric juicers. Handheld squeezers are available in different sizes, and often painted to match their intended fruit—green for limes, yellow for lemons, and orange for, well, oranges. If you purchase just one, choose the largest size, as it will fit all kinds of citrus.

Pastry Blender: Also known as a pastry knife, this reliable tool features multiple thin, dull blades arranged in an arch shape attached to a wide, sturdy handle. It is used to cut butter into flour for piecrusts like Bourbon Peach Pie Bars (page 216), and crumble toppings like On-the-Go Blueberry Breakfast Bars (page 196). If a pastry blender isn't available, use two butter knives, or even your fingers, to work the butter into the flour and achieve similar results.

Mortar and Pestle: Humans have prepared ingredients with mortars and pestles since the Stone Age. In this book, these ancient tools are used for grinding spices and crushing ingredients like the hard candies in our Sour Lemon Stained-Glass Stars (page 128). If a mortar and pestle isn't available, place ingredients in a plastic zip-top bag and crush them with a rolling pin.

Kitchen Torch: This small kitchen tool is used only once in this book. With a powerful, focused flame, it quickly torches the tops of our caramelized Crème Brûlée Cookies (page 256). Kitchen torches are inexpensive and available in kitchen supply stores and online.

Measuring Tools

Liquid Measuring Cups: When purchasing liquid measuring cups, avoid plastic varieties, and instead look for brands made of Pyrex glass. This heatproof material allows for safely measuring boiling water and other hot ingredients. We recommend having several sizes of cups—at least a 1 cup, 2 cup, and 4 cup—to accurately measure liquid ingredients of different amounts.

Dry Measuring Cups: You'll rarely use dry measuring cups if you own a digital kitchen scale, since scales are the most accurate way to measure dry ingredients (see Digital Scales on page 8). If you prefer to use measuring cups, look for metal varieties, since plastic can discolor and accumulate odors over time. A basic set includes ¼ cup, ⅓ cup, ½ cup, ⅔ cup, ¾ cup, and 1 cup, and often has larger sizes like 1½ cups and 2 cups.

Measuring Spoons: A set of measuring spoons includes ⅛ teaspoon, ¼ teaspoon, ½ teaspoon, ¾ teaspoon, 1 teaspoon, ½ tablespoon, and 1 tablespoon. When purchasing, look for spoons that are long and thin—if the spoons are round and wide, they won't fit inside small spice bottles.

Kitchen Timer: A digital kitchen timer is less essential since the smartphones in our pockets have built-in timers, but owning an additional portable timer to keep on the counter is helpful for baking, especially when multitasking.

Cooking Thermometer: There are two common types of cooking thermometers: candy thermometers and probe thermometers. Candy thermometers, also known as deep-fry thermometers, feature a clip on the side, allowing them to attach to a simmering pot so you can constantly monitor the temperature while your ingredients cook. They are useful when heating caramels and custards that require a specific temperature. If you don't have a candy thermometer, you can use a probe thermometer instead. These handheld tools feature a thin metal probe, which is inserted into simmering ingredients to check the temperature. They aren't as convenient as hands-free, clip-on candy thermometers, but they measure temperature just as accurately.

Baking Pans

Baking Sheet: The most common and versatile baking sheet is a half sheet pan, which measures 18 x 13 inches and features raised 1-inch sides. The raised sides prevent liquids from leaking during baking, making them preferable to traditional cookie sheets, which are flat pans with a raised edge on just one side. Look for pans made of stainless steel, rather than nonstick pans, which scratch easily and are less durable.

13 x 9-inch Baking Dish: This versatile dish is the perfect size to bake bar cookies and brownies. They are available in ceramic, oven-safe glass, or metal varieties, and they all work equally well. Avoid nonstick bakeware, as they are susceptible to scratching and need to be replaced more often. Note that when you line your pans with parchment paper, sticking is never an issue (see Using Parchment Paper on page 7).

8-inch Square Baking Dish: Square pans are used in this book for small-batch bar cookies, like our Peanut Butter Pretzel Fudge Bars (page 210). An 8-inch square pan is approximately half the size of a 13 x 9-inch pan, so anytime a half recipe of brownies or bars is desired, simply use half the amount of each ingredient. The baking time may vary slightly, but the end result will be the same.

Mini Cupcake Pan: While standard cupcake pans have 12 large cups, mini cupcake pans have 24 mini cups, making them perfect for baking miniature treats. This inexpensive and handy pan is used in only one recipe in this book, but if you don't own one, you may consider adding it to your collection, otherwise you'll just have to imagine what our dreamy Cannoli Cookie Cups (page 242) taste like.

Decoration Tools

Cookie Cutters: There are countless styles of cookie cutters available, from simple geometric shapes to elaborate holiday designs. Anytime a recipe in this book suggests a cookie shape, feel free to substitute another shape of your choice—note that changing the shape or size may affect the cooking time, so be sure to monitor the cookies while they bake.

All the recipes in this book that utilize cookie cutters can be made with the following shapes:

- 1½-INCH CIRCLE

- 2-INCH CIRCLE

- 2½-INCH CIRCLE

- 3-INCH CIRCLE

- 2½-INCH RUFFLED CIRCLE

- 1-INCH SQUARE

- 2½-INCH RUFFLED SQUARE

- 1-INCH HEART

- 3-INCH HEART

- 1-INCH STAR

- 3-INCH STAR

- 3-INCH OVAL

- 3-INCH PEOPLE

Piping Bag: Also known as pastry bags, these kitchen tools are used in this book to decorate and fill cookies. They are designed to draw thin lines of frosting, pipe perfect meringues and marshmallows, and create star-shaped treats like Cinnamon Sugar Churro Cookies (page 244). While piping bags have an endless selection of tips in various shapes and sizes, you will only need three tips for the recipes in this book—a small round tip, a wide round tip, and an open star tip. If piping bags are unavailable, use a zip-top plastic bag with one corner cut off.

Pastry Brush: Pastry brushes are useful for applying egg washes and thin glazes on cookies. When purchasing, look for silicone brushes, as natural brushes can shed unwanted fibers.

Paintbrush: You will use a paintbrush only once in this book—to create delicate lines of color for our Citrus Meringue Drops (page 122). A small, clean craft paintbrush will work perfectly for this application. Be sure to keep baking brushes separate from paintbrushes, and never prepare food with a brush that was previously used for paint.

Other

Mixing Bowls: Every home cook or baker should own a set of mixing bowls in various sizes. When purchasing, look for heatproof Pyrex glass bowls—these sturdy, damage-resistant bowls can be heated in the microwave, baked in the oven, and placed above a simmering pot of water to create a double boiler. Avoid buying plastic mixing bowls, as they are not heatproof and can degrade over time.

Wire Racks: You will use wire racks for almost every recipe in this book. Wire racks allow for proper air circulation, which helps freshly baked cookies retain their delicate texture as they cool. Some racks are available in sets that can be stacked vertically, which saves counter space when cooling large numbers of cookies at once.

Plastic Wrap: This thin, plastic film is commonly used to seal and secure food items in containers. Since plastic wrap is airtight and watertight, it is perfect for keeping cookie dough fresh in the fridge. It's also useful for storing custards—press the plastic wrap directly onto the surface of the custard, which will prevent a skin from forming.

We wanted to
make things easy for
you. To purchase any of
the specialty ingredients,
tools, and equipment used
in this book, scan the
QR code below.

▼

Gluten-Free Recipes

Nearly every recipe in this book can be made gluten-free by using a gluten-free flour blend instead of all-purpose flour (see Gluten-Free Baking on page 8 for more info). The following recipes don't contain any gluten or flour at all.

Dark Chocolate Peanut Butter Truffles (page 60)

Quick Butterscotch Pralines (page 62)

5-Ingredient Peanut Butter Blossoms (page 76)

Citrus Meringue Drops (page 122)

Lemon Olive Oil Pignoli (page 152)

Chocolate Brigadeiro Truffles (page 182)

Hibiscus Suspiro Meringues (page 187)

Crispy Triple Chocolate Marshmallow Treats (page 222)

Flourless Chocolate Cake Cookies (page 254)

Dairy-Free Recipes

Almost all of the recipes in this book can easily be made dairy-free by substituting a nondairy butter. These six recipes are naturally dairy-free.

No-Bake Tropical Rum Balls (page 74)

Citrus Meringue Drops (page 122)

Lemon Olive Oil Pignoli (page 152)

Melomakarona Spiced Honey Cookies (page 159)

Hibiscus Suspiro Meringues (page 187)

Flourless Chocolate Cake Cookies (page 254)

Quick and Easy Recipes

These are the quickest recipes in the book—for when you need a cookie, and you need one now.

the fab five

(An energized audience cheers.) "Never before have the world's taste buds felt such excitement, stirred by these first five cookies who call themselves The Fab Five. Hundreds of reporters from all over the nation have been anxiously waiting outside our kitchen for us to announce these recipes, and today everything will be revealed. From The Perfect Chocolate Chip Cookie (page 44) to Vanilla Bean Sugar Cookies (page 43), this chapter includes five cookie staples that should be in every baker's repertoire. Cookiemania is sweeping the globe, uniting humanity into one cookie community . . . and That Takes the Cookie. Get ready—we have a really big show tonight. Ladies and gentlemen, The Fab Five!"

2½ cups (300 g) all-purpose flour

1 teaspoon baking soda

¾ teaspoon salt

½ teaspoon baking powder

1 vanilla bean

2 sticks (226 g) unsalted butter,
at room temperature

1¾ cups (347 g) granulated sugar,
plus more for rolling

1 large egg, at room temperature

2 teaspoons vanilla extract

Note: The empty vanilla bean
pod can be discarded or used
in a bottle of homemade
vanilla extract (page 18).

Vanilla Bean Sugar Cookies

The next time your cookie cravings call for something
simple yet glamorous, this effortless recipe will dazzle
your dreams. With a noticeably crisp crunch and a tender,
buttery interior, these delectable cookies glisten in their
sparkly sugar coats stylishly speckled with real vanilla
beans. Easy to prepare and always the life of the party, The
Fab Five wouldn't be complete without this shining star.

Make the Dough: In a small bowl, whisk together the
flour, baking soda, salt, and baking powder. Set aside.

Use a small, sharp knife to cut the vanilla bean in half
lengthwise. Then use the back of the knife to scrape out all
the seeds and set them aside. Discard the bean pod or save it
for another use (see note).

In a large mixing bowl, beat the butter and sugar on medium
speed until light and fluffy. Add the vanilla seeds, egg, and
vanilla extract and beat until smooth. Add the flour mixture
and beat until no dry streaks remain. Cover the bowl with
plastic and refrigerate for at least 2 hours. Dough can keep
in the fridge for up to 1 week.

Bake the Cookies: Preheat the oven to 350°F (177°C) and
line one or more baking sheets with parchment paper.

Pour a few tablespoons of granulated sugar into a small
bowl, then set aside.

Scoop about 1 tablespoon dough into a ball, then roll it in
the bowl of sugar until evenly coated and sparkling. Place it
on the prepared baking sheet, then repeat with the remaining dough, leaving 2 inches of space between each one and
placing approximately 12 dough balls per sheet.

Bake for 10 to 12 minutes, until the edges are lightly golden
and the centers no longer appear wet. If baking two pans
at once, swap the positions of the pans halfway through to
ensure the cookies bake evenly.

Let the cookies cool on the baking sheet for 5 minutes, then
transfer to a wire rack to cool completely. Enjoy!

2½ cups (300 g) all-purpose flour

1 teaspoon baking soda

1 teaspoon salt

2 sticks (226 g) unsalted butter, at room temperature

1 cup (213 g) brown sugar

¾ cup (149 g) granulated sugar

2 large eggs, at room temperature

2 tablespoons creamy unsalted almond butter

2 teaspoons vanilla extract

2 cups (340 g) semisweet chocolate chips

The Perfect Chocolate Chip Cookie

We know what you're thinking. How could we declare these as "perfect" when there are countless chocolate chip cookie recipes out there already? Well, you're just going to have to try it yourself—the proof is in the cookie. This monumental cookie earns the moniker "perfect"— it's crispy on the outside, magnificently chewy on the inside, and features a special ingredient that sets it apart from its cookie competitors. Our secret is simple—a spoonful of creamy almond butter. This tasty technique adds a subtle hint of nuttiness while contributing to its noteworthy chew. When enjoyed warm from the oven, after one bite you, too, will be proclaiming that this truly is The Perfect Chocolate Chip Cookie.

Make the Dough: In a small bowl, whisk together the flour, baking soda, and salt. Set aside.

In a large mixing bowl, beat the butter, brown sugar, and granulated sugar on medium speed until light and fluffy. Add the eggs, almond butter, and vanilla and beat until smooth. Add the flour mixture and beat until no dry streaks remain. Add the chocolate chips, then stir by hand until evenly distributed in the dough. Cover the bowl with plastic and refrigerate for at least 2 hours. Dough can keep in the fridge for up to 1 week.

Bake the Cookies: Preheat the oven to 375°F (190°C) and line one or more baking sheets with parchment paper.

Scoop about 2 tablespoons dough into a ball and place it on the prepared baking sheet. Repeat with the remaining dough, leaving 2 inches of space between each one and placing approximately 12 dough balls per sheet.

Bake for 9 to 11 minutes, until the edges are golden and the centers no longer appear wet. If baking two pans at once, swap the positions of the pans halfway through to ensure the cookies bake evenly.

Let the cookies cool on the baking sheet for 5 minutes, then transfer to a wire rack to cool completely. Enjoy!

Classic Gingerbread Cookies

3½ cups (420 g) all-purpose flour, plus more for dusting

1 tablespoon ground ginger

2 teaspoons ground cinnamon

1 teaspoon baking soda

½ teaspoon salt

½ teaspoon ground cloves

½ teaspoon ground allspice

1½ sticks (170 g) unsalted butter, at room temperature

¾ cup (160 g) brown sugar

1 large egg, at room temperature

¾ cup (255 g) molasses

1 teaspoon vanilla extract

The hills are alive with the scent of gingerbread! Overflowing with cinnamon, ginger, cloves, and allspice, these cookies are buzzing with flavor. With crispy edges and a soft center, they deserve to be more than just a once-a-year Christmas treat—try shaping them into romantic hearts for Valentine's Day or cut out spooky ghosts for Halloween. If you love gingerbread as much as we do, you'll find reasons to make this classic cookie all year long.

Make the Dough: In a small bowl, whisk together the flour, ginger, cinnamon, baking soda, salt, cloves, and allspice. Set aside.

In a large mixing bowl, beat the butter and brown sugar on medium speed until light and fluffy. Add the egg, molasses, and vanilla and beat until smooth. Add the flour mixture and beat until no dry streaks remain. Gather the dough, then divide in half. Roll each half into a ball, wrap tightly in plastic, then flatten slightly to make a disc shape and refrigerate for at least 2 hours. Dough can keep in the fridge for up to 1 week.

Bake the Cookies: Preheat the oven to 350°F (177°C).

Since this dough is fairly sticky, it is best to roll it between two sheets of parchment paper. First, place a 16-inch square of parchment on the countertop and lightly dust it with flour. Unwrap one of the discs of dough, place it in the center of the parchment, and lightly dust the top of the dough with flour. Place another 16-inch square of parchment on top of the dough and use a rolling pin to flatten the dough between the two pieces of parchment until it makes a large circle approximately ¼ inch thick. If the dough begins to stick to the parchment while rolling, lift the parchment and dust the dough with flour before continuing. Once the dough is rolled ¼ inch thick, use the parchment to lift the flattened circle of dough onto a baking sheet. Place the baking sheet in the freezer for 15 minutes; this will firm up the dough and ensures clean cutout shapes. Repeat the process with the second disc of dough.

Remove the baking sheet from the freezer and use the parchment to lift the dough onto the countertop. Using cookie cutter shapes of your choice, cut out as many shapes as possible, dipping the cookie cutter in flour between cuts to prevent sticking, if needed. Transfer the cookie shapes to a parchment-lined baking sheet, leaving about 1 inch of space between each one. Repeat with the second circle of dough. Gather and reroll the dough scraps, then cut out the remaining cookies, using additional baking sheets as needed. Place the baking sheets in the freezer for 15 minutes; this helps the cookies keep their shape while baking.

Transfer the baking sheets directly to the oven and bake for 9 to 11 minutes, until the edges of the cookies begin to darken slightly and the centers no longer appear wet. If baking two pans at once, swap the positions of the pans halfway through to ensure the cookies bake evenly.

Let the cookies cool on the baking sheet for 5 minutes, then transfer to a wire rack to cool completely. Enjoy!

2 sticks (226 g) unsalted butter,
at room temperature

½ cup (99 g) granulated sugar

½ teaspoon salt

1 teaspoon vanilla extract

2 cups (240 g) all-purpose flour,
plus more for dusting

Note: To create a traditional
shortbread design, skip the
decorative rolling pin and
use a chopstick or wooden
dowel to poke several holes
on each cookie after placing
them on the baking sheet.

Buttery Shortbread Cookies

Attention: please proceed with caution. These cookies
are dangerously easy to make, and all five ingredients are
probably in your kitchen at this very moment. If you have
flour, sugar, salt, butter, and vanilla, then today is your
lucky day. Often, shortbread can be dry and flavorless, but
this powerfully addicting version is intensely buttery and
melt-in-your-mouth marvelous.

Make the Dough: In a large mixing bowl, beat the butter,
sugar, and salt on medium speed until light and fluffy. Add
the vanilla and beat until smooth. Add the flour and beat
until no dry streaks remain. Gather the dough into a ball,
then flatten slightly to make a disc shape. Wrap tightly in
plastic and refrigerate for at least 2 hours. Dough can keep
in the fridge for up to 1 week.

Bake the Cookies: Preheat the oven to 350°F (177°C) and
line one or more baking sheets with parchment paper.

Unwrap the disc of dough and place it on a lightly floured
work surface. Roll the dough to a large circle about ½ inch
thick. The dough may crack slightly, so if this happens, gently press it back together as you roll. If desired, use a decorative rolling pin to create a pattern on the surface of the
dough. Using the cookie cutter shapes of your choice, cut
out as many shapes as possible from the dough. Transfer the
cookie shapes to the prepared baking sheets, leaving about
1 inch of space between each cookie. Gather and reroll the
dough scraps, then cut out the remaining cookies. Place the
baking sheets in the freezer for 15 minutes; this helps the
cookies keep their shape while baking.

Transfer the baking sheets directly to the oven and bake for
12 to 14 minutes, until the edges of the cookies are lightly
golden and the centers no longer appear wet. If baking two
pans at once, swap the positions of the pans halfway through
to ensure the cookies bake evenly.

Let the cookies cool on the baking sheet for 5 minutes, then
transfer to a wire rack to cool completely. Enjoy!

1½ cups (180 g) all-purpose flour

1 teaspoon baking soda

1 teaspoon ground cinnamon

½ teaspoon salt

¼ teaspoon ground nutmeg

1 stick (113 g) unsalted butter,
at room temperature

1 cup (213 g) brown sugar

½ cup (99 g) granulated sugar

2 large eggs, at room temperature

2 teaspoons vanilla extract

1½ cups (225 g) raisins

3 cups (267 g) rolled oats

Chewy Oatmeal Raisin Cookies

If you consider yourself a Chocolate Chip Cookie Person and were planning to skip past this page, we urge you to stay and continue reading these important and potentially life-changing words. These ultrachewy cookies are persuasively spiced with cinnamon, nutmeg, brown sugar, and vanilla, and loaded with plump raisins and rolled oats. Powerful enough to make anyone a cookie convert, we'd like to present your new favorite cookie. Hashtag #NoChocolateChipsNeeded

Make the Dough: In a small bowl, whisk together the flour, baking soda, cinnamon, salt, and nutmeg. Set aside.

In a large mixing bowl, beat the butter, brown sugar, and granulated sugar on medium speed until light and fluffy. Add the eggs and vanilla and beat until smooth. Add the flour mixture and beat until no dry streaks remain. Add the raisins and oats, and stir by hand until evenly distributed in the dough. Cover the bowl with plastic and refrigerate for at least 2 hours. Dough can keep in the fridge for up to 1 week.

Bake the Cookies: Preheat the oven to 350°F (177°C) and line one or more baking sheets with parchment paper.

Scoop about 2 tablespoons dough into a ball and place it on the prepared baking sheet. Repeat with the remaining dough, leaving 2 inches of space between each one and placing approximately 12 dough balls per sheet.

Bake for 12 to 14 minutes, until the edges are golden and the centers no longer appear wet. If baking two pans at once, swap the positions of the pans halfway through to ensure the cookies bake evenly.

Let the cookies cool on the baking sheet for 5 minutes, then transfer to a wire rack to cool completely. Enjoy!

chapter 2

classics
with a
twist

Some of the best stories use unexpected plot twists to keep you on your toes and catch you off guard—like the iconic moment when Darth Vader reveals Luke Skywalker's true parentage in *The Empire Strikes Back*. The same goes for cookies. This chapter is filled with delicious twists and unforeseen turns like our Pumpkin Pie Thumbprints (page 58), Maple-Walnut Florentines (page 67), and Chai-Spiced Wedding Cookies (page 64). Prepare your palate for an adventure of flavor where mouthwatering mysteries hide within every page. These clever cookies are guaranteed to keep you on the edge of your seat, and That Takes the Cookie.

Slice-and-Bake Cinnamon Roll Cookies

For the Cookies

2¼ cups (270 g) all-purpose flour

½ teaspoon baking powder

½ teaspoon salt

2 sticks (226 g) unsalted butter, at room temperature

¾ cup (149 g) granulated sugar

1 large egg, at room temperature

1 teaspoon vanilla extract

For the Cinnamon–Brown Sugar Filling

¼ cup (54 g) brown sugar

2¼ teaspoons ground cinnamon

2 tablespoons unsalted butter, melted and cooled slightly

For the Vanilla Glaze

½ cup (57 g) powdered sugar

2 teaspoons milk of your choice, plus more if needed

¼ teaspoon vanilla extract

Breakfast is served! This is our favorite cinnamon roll recipe, transformed into an unforgettable cookie. Rolled with a buttery, cinnamon–brown sugar filling and delicately drizzled with vanilla glaze, these soft cookies begin to caramelize underneath as they bake, giving them an irresistible crunch. Try dipping one in a cup of coffee, and your mornings will never be the same.

Make the Dough: In a small bowl, whisk together the flour, baking powder, and salt. Set aside.

In a large mixing bowl, beat the butter and granulated sugar on medium speed until light and fluffy. Add the egg and 1 teaspoon vanilla and beat until smooth. Add the flour mixture and beat until no dry streaks remain. Gather the dough, then divide in half. Form each half into a brick shape, then flatten slightly to about 1 inch thick. Wrap tightly in plastic and refrigerate for at least 2 hours. Dough can keep in the fridge for up to 1 week.

Make the Filling and Roll the Dough: In a small bowl, stir together the brown sugar and cinnamon until evenly blended with no clumps remaining.

Unwrap one of the rectangles of dough and place it on a lightly floured work surface. Roll the dough to a 9 x 7-inch rectangle about ¼ inch thick. The dough may crack slightly, so if this happens, gently press it back together as you roll. Using a knife or pizza cutter, trim the edges to make a clean rectangular shape, and discard the excess dough. Brush the dough with a small amount of melted butter until lightly moistened—you will not use all the butter. Sprinkle half the cinnamon-sugar mixture over the dough, leaving ¼ inch of space around the edges. Carefully roll the dough tightly into a 9-inch log about 2 inches thick, then wrap in plastic.

Repeat with the second half of dough and the remaining cinnamon-sugar filling. Place the two logs seam side down in the refrigerator for at least 1 hour. Dough can keep in the fridge for up to 1 week.

Bake the Cookies: Preheat the oven to 350°F (177°C) and line one or more baking sheets with parchment paper.

Unwrap one of the logs of dough, and if the bottom has flattened a bit, gently squeeze the log until it becomes a perfect cylinder. Use a sharp knife to slice the log into ½-inch-thick circles. Place the circles on the prepared baking sheet, leaving 2 inches of space between each one and placing approximately 15 circles per sheet. Repeat with the remaining dough. Place the baking sheets in the freezer for 15 minutes; this helps the cookies keep their shape while baking.

Transfer the baking sheets directly to the oven and bake for 10 to 12 minutes, until the edges are golden. If baking two pans at once, swap the positions of the pans halfway through to ensure the cookies bake evenly.

Let the cookies cool on the baking sheet for 5 minutes, then transfer to a wire rack to cool completely.

Glaze the Cookies: In a small bowl, stir together the powdered sugar, milk, and ¼ teaspoon vanilla until smooth and creamy, adding more milk if needed to thin.

Drizzle the cookies with the glaze, using about ½ teaspoon per cookie. The glazed cookies will dry in about 20 minutes. Enjoy!

2½ cups (300 g) all-purpose flour

1 teaspoon baking soda

1 teaspoon salt

½ teaspoon baking powder

2 sticks (226 g) unsalted butter,
at room temperature

¾ cup (160 g) brown sugar

¾ cup (149 g) granulated sugar

2 large eggs, at room temperature

1 tablespoon grated orange zest
(from 1 large orange)

2 teaspoons vanilla extract

2 cups (340 g) white chocolate
chips

1½ cups (210 g) dried cranberries

Cranberry-Orange White Chocolate Chip Cookies

If there were Academy Awards for cookies, this aspiring nominee would win the Oscar for Cookie of the Year. Reveling down the red carpet with classy white chocolate chips and colorful dried cranberries, this eye-catching cookie has zest-to-impress. Featuring tangy orange zest in the dough, this chewy champion comes with a blast of citrus and an award-winning flavor combination. Coming soon to an oven near you.

Make the Dough: In a small bowl, whisk together the flour, baking soda, salt, and baking powder. Set aside.

In a large mixing bowl, beat the butter, brown sugar, and granulated sugar on medium speed until light and fluffy. Add the eggs, orange zest, and vanilla and beat until smooth. Add the flour mixture and beat until no dry streaks remain. Next, add the white chocolate chips and cranberries, then stir by hand until evenly distributed in the dough. Cover the bowl with plastic and refrigerate for at least 2 hours. Dough can keep in the fridge for up to 1 week.

Bake the Cookies: Preheat the oven to 350°F (177°C) and line one or more baking sheets with parchment paper.

Scoop about 2 tablespoons dough into a ball and place it on the prepared baking sheet. Repeat with the remaining dough, leaving 2 inches of space between each one and placing approximately 12 dough balls per sheet.

Bake for 12 to 14 minutes, until the edges are golden and the centers no longer appear wet. If baking two pans at once, swap the positions of the pans halfway through to ensure the cookies bake evenly.

Let the cookies cool on the baking sheet for 5 minutes, then transfer to a wire rack to cool completely. Enjoy!

30 to 32 (2-inch) cookies

Pumpkin Pie Thumbprints

For the Cookies

2¼ cups (270 g) all-purpose flour

½ teaspoon baking powder

½ teaspoon salt

2 sticks (226 g) unsalted butter, at room temperature

¾ cup (149 g) granulated sugar

1 large egg, at room temperature

1 teaspoon vanilla extract

For the Pumpkin Pie Filling

1 cup (226 g) canned pumpkin puree

¼ cup (50 g) granulated sugar

2 tablespoons plus 2 teaspoons brown sugar

½ teaspoon ground cinnamon

½ teaspoon ground ginger

¼ teaspoon ground nutmeg

¼ teaspoon salt

⅛ teaspoon ground allspice

Calling all fall flavor lovers! Your dreams have come true. We're about to change your life with this buttery thumbprint cookie. Astonish your guests and expand their minds by bringing these adorable mini-pie-like cookies to the table. With a smooth pumpkin pie filling that tastes like Thanksgiving, we encourage you to try them chilled and topped with a dollop of whipped cream. Feel free to pinch yourself after your first bite—you're not dreaming.

Make the Dough: In a small bowl, whisk together the flour, baking powder, and ½ teaspoon salt. Set aside.

In a large mixing bowl, beat the butter and ¾ cup granulated sugar on medium speed until light and fluffy. Add the egg and vanilla and beat until smooth. Add the flour mixture and beat until no dry streaks remain. Cover the bowl with plastic and refrigerate for at least 2 hours. Dough can keep in the fridge for up to 1 week.

Make the Filling: In a small bowl, combine the pumpkin puree, ¼ cup granulated sugar, brown sugar, cinnamon, ginger, nutmeg, ¼ teaspoon salt, and allspice. Stir until evenly blended. Keep covered in the refrigerator until ready to use.

Bake the Cookies: Preheat the oven to 350°F (177°C) and line one or more baking sheets with parchment paper.

Scoop 1 tablespoon dough into a ball and place it on the prepared baking sheet. Repeat with the remaining dough, leaving 2 inches of space between each one and placing approximately 12 dough balls per sheet. Use your thumb to create a well in the center of each cookie large enough to hold 1½ teaspoons pumpkin filling. Spoon 1½ teaspoons pumpkin filling into the center of each cookie. Place the baking sheets in the freezer for 15 minutes; this helps the cookies keep their shape while baking.

Transfer the baking sheets directly to the oven and bake for 12 to 14 minutes, until the edges are golden. If baking two pans at once, swap the positions of the pans halfway through to ensure the cookies bake evenly.

Let the cookies cool on the baking sheet for 5 minutes, then transfer to a wire rack to cool completely. Enjoy!

Note: If desired, serve these cookies chilled and topped with a dollop of whipped cream.

Makes

30 to 32
(1-inch)
truffles

Gluten-Free

2 cups (226 g) powdered sugar, sifted

¾ cup plus 2 tablespoons (226 g) no-stir creamy peanut butter

1 stick (113 g) unsalted butter, at room temperature

¼ teaspoon salt

1⅓ cups (226 g) semisweet chocolate chips (about 45% cacao)

1⅓ cups (226 g) bittersweet chocolate chips (about 65% cacao)

2 teaspoons coconut oil (see note)

Dark Chocolate Peanut Butter Truffles

You may want to sit down while you read this—we bring some exciting news. Did you know that you can easily make peanut butter cups at home? It's true! There's no oven needed to prepare these gourmet truffles, and they make wonderful gifts . . . if you're willing to share, that is. With a crisp, candy-like dark chocolate shell and an intensely creamy peanut butter middle, you are one bite away from experiencing chocolate peanut butter bliss.

Make the Filling: In a large mixing bowl, beat the powdered sugar, peanut butter, butter, and salt on medium speed until light and fluffy. Cover the bowl with plastic and refrigerate for at least 2 hours. Filling can keep in the fridge for up to 1 week.

Dip the Truffles: Line a baking sheet with parchment paper. Scoop 1 tablespoon filling into a ball and place it on the prepared baking sheet. Repeat with the remaining dough, leaving 1 inch of space between each one. Place the baking sheet in the freezer for 15 minutes; this helps the truffles keep their shape while dipping.

Fill a small saucepan with 1 to 2 inches of water, and bring to a simmer over medium heat. Place a small heatproof bowl over the pan, so the bottom of the bowl rests above the surface of the simmering water. Place the semisweet chips, bittersweet chips, and coconut oil in the bowl and stir until melted and smooth with no lumps remaining. Turn the heat as low as possible to keep the chocolate warm.

Remove the baking sheet from the freezer and set it next to the stove. Using a toothpick or fork, pick up one of the frozen truffles. Coat it completely in melted chocolate, either by dipping the truffle, or by holding it over the bowl and drizzling spoonfuls of melted chocolate over it, allowing the excess chocolate to drip back into the bowl. Place the coated truffle back onto the parchment-lined baking sheet.

Remove the toothpick and use it to smooth over the hole. Repeat with the remaining truffles until all have been coated in chocolate. During the process, if the truffles begin to warm and soften, transfer the sheet back to the freezer for a few minutes so the truffles firm up. Once all the truffles have been coated in chocolate, place the baking sheet in the refrigerator for 1 hour. Transfer the truffles to a sealed container and keep refrigerated. Serve chilled, and enjoy!

Note: Either refined coconut oil or virgin coconut oil will work for this recipe.

1 cup (113 g) pecans

1 cup plus 1 tablespoon (226 g)
brown sugar

½ cup (118 ml) heavy cream

4 tablespoons (57 g) unsalted
butter

¼ teaspoon salt

½ cup (85 g) butterscotch chips

1 teaspoon vanilla extract

Quick Butterscotch Pralines

If you've never tried a praline, let this simple recipe be
your first. Softer than a cookie and smooth like fudge,
these creamy confections are super easy to make, cooked
in just minutes on the stovetop with toasted pecans, melted
butterscotch chips, brown sugar, and cream. If you need
a cookie—like right now—these golden beauties are the
quickest in the book.

Scatter the pecans in a dry skillet and place over medium
heat. Cook, stirring occasionally, until toasted and fragrant,
5 to 7 minutes. Transfer to a heatproof plate and set in the
freezer for 5 minutes to cool. Finely chop the pecans, then
set aside.

Line a baking sheet with parchment paper.

In a medium saucepan, combine the brown sugar, heavy
cream, butter, and salt. Set over medium heat and cook,
stirring often, until the mixture begins to simmer. Insert a
cooking thermometer and continue to cook and stir until
the mixture reaches 240°F (116°C). Then turn off the heat,
add the pecans, butterscotch chips, and vanilla and stir vigorously to combine. Use a spoon to scoop about 1 tablespoon
hot caramel mixture onto the prepared baking sheet, working quickly before the caramel cools and hardens. Repeat
with the remaining caramel, leaving 1 inch of space between
each one.

Let the pralines cool on the baking sheet for 30 minutes,
then transfer to a wire rack to cool completely. Enjoy!

¾ cup (85 g) pecans

2¼ cups (270 g) all-purpose flour

2 teaspoons ground cinnamon

1 teaspoon ground ginger

½ teaspoon salt

¼ teaspoon ground nutmeg

¼ teaspoon ground cardamom

¼ teaspoon ground allspice

⅛ teaspoon ground cloves

Pinch of freshly ground black pepper

2 sticks (226 g) unsalted butter, at room temperature

½ cup (57 g) powdered sugar, sifted, plus more for rolling

2 teaspoons vanilla extract

Chai-Spiced Wedding Cookies

This recipe is a party in a cookie! Also known as Russian tea cakes, these soft and crumbly cookies are bejeweled with toasted pecans and rolled in powdered sugar. To elevate this popular pastry, our version is filled with an aromatic masala chai spice blend of cinnamon, ginger, nutmeg, cardamom, cloves, and allspice. Traditionally served at holidays and weddings, this lively cookie is a cause for celebration in itself.

Make the Dough: Scatter the pecans in a dry skillet and place over medium heat. Cook, stirring occasionally, until toasted and fragrant, 5 to 7 minutes. Transfer to a heatproof plate and set in the freezer for 5 minutes to cool. Finely chop the pecans, then set aside.

In a small bowl, whisk together the flour, cinnamon, ginger, salt, nutmeg, cardamom, allspice, cloves, and black pepper. Set aside.

In a large mixing bowl, beat the butter and powdered sugar on medium speed until light and fluffy. Add the vanilla and beat until smooth. Add the flour mixture and beat until no dry streaks remain. Next, add the pecans, then stir by hand until evenly distributed in the dough. Cover the bowl with plastic and refrigerate for at least 2 hours. Dough can keep in the fridge for up to 1 week.

Bake the Cookies: Preheat the oven to 350°F (177°C) and line one or more baking sheets with parchment paper.

Scoop about 1 tablespoon dough into a ball and place it on the prepared baking sheet. Repeat with the remaining dough, leaving 2 inches of space between each one and placing approximately 12 dough balls per sheet.

Bake for 16 to 18 minutes, until the edges are golden. If baking two pans at once, swap the positions of the pans halfway through to ensure the cookies bake evenly.

Continued . . .

Let the cookies cool on the baking sheet for 5 minutes. While the cookies are cooling, fill a wide, shallow bowl with powdered sugar.

Once the cookies have cooled, carefully pick one up (it will still be hot, so use tongs if necessary) and roll it in the bowl of powdered sugar until evenly coated in a thick layer. Place the cookie on a wire rack and repeat with the remaining cookies. Let the cookies cool completely, 45 to 60 minutes. Once completely cool, roll each cookie in powdered sugar again until evenly coated. Enjoy!

Makes 22 to 24 (3-inch) cookies

For the Cookies

1 cup (113 g) walnuts

1½ tablespoons all-purpose flour

⅛ teaspoon salt

6 tablespoons (75 g) granulated sugar

3 tablespoons unsalted butter

1½ tablespoons heavy cream

1 tablespoon maple syrup

¼ teaspoon vanilla extract

For the Maple Glaze

½ cup (57 g) powdered sugar, sifted

2 tablespoons plus 2 teaspoons maple syrup

Generous pinch of salt

Maple-Walnut Florentines

Alert the press—there's a new cookie in town. Traditionally, Florentine lace cookies are coated with chocolate, but we discovered something even better. Drizzled in a doughnut-inspired maple glaze, these thin and delicate cookies are crispy, chewy, and magnificently maple-y. Baked with toasted walnuts, vanilla, and sweetened with real maple syrup, this recipe will be making all the headlines.

Make the Dough: Scatter the walnuts in a dry skillet and place over medium heat. Cook, stirring occasionally, until toasted and fragrant, 5 to 7 minutes. Transfer to a heatproof plate and set in the freezer for 5 minutes to cool.

In a food processor, pulse the walnuts until coarsely chopped. Add the flour and ⅛ teaspoon salt and pulse until evenly combined and sandy-textured. Set aside.

In a medium saucepan, combine the granulated sugar, butter, heavy cream, and maple syrup. Set over medium heat and cook, stirring often, until the mixture begins to simmer. Continue cooking for 1 minute, until the sugar is completely dissolved. Remove from the heat and add the flour mixture and vanilla, stirring to combine. Transfer to a heatproof bowl and let cool at room temperature for 15 to 20 minutes. You can then bake the dough immediately, or cover with plastic and keep refrigerated until ready to bake.

Bake the Cookies: Preheat the oven to 350°F (177°C) and line one or more baking sheets with parchment paper.

Scoop 1 heaping teaspoon dough into a ball and place it on the prepared baking sheet—if the chilled dough is too firm to roll, allow it to rest at room temperature for a few minutes until softened. Repeat with the remaining dough, leaving 3 inches of space between each one and placing approximately 12 dough balls per baking sheet.

Continued...

Bake for 10 to 12 minutes, until the edges are deeply golden. The center of the cookies may look soft, but they will harden as they cool. If baking two pans at once, swap the positions of the pans halfway through to ensure the cookies bake evenly.

Let the cookies cool on the baking sheet for 5 minutes, then transfer to a wire rack to cool completely.

Glaze the Cookies: In a small bowl, stir together the powdered sugar, maple syrup, and a pinch of salt until smooth and creamy.

Drizzle the cookies with the maple glaze, using about ½ teaspoon per cookie. The glazed cookies will dry in about 20 minutes. Enjoy!

Makes

**24
(3-inch)
cookies**

3 cups (360 g) all-purpose flour

1 tablespoon ground ginger

2½ teaspoons ground cinnamon

¾ teaspoon baking soda

½ teaspoon salt

½ teaspoon ground cloves

½ teaspoon ground allspice

¼ teaspoon ground nutmeg

1½ sticks (170 g) unsalted butter,
at room temperature

¾ cup (160 g) brown sugar

½ cup (170 g) molasses

2 tablespoons milk of your choice

Granulated sugar, for rolling

Powdered sugar, for rolling

Gingerbread Crinkles

Magic Mirror on the wall, who is the chewiest cookie
of all? The answer will be clear when you make these
crinkles—they're the chewiest in the land. We combined a
symphony of spices to make an intense gingerbread cookie
that's animated with flavor. With a fudgy, brownie-like
texture and dramatic crackled-sugar top, all it takes is
one bite and you'll be whistling while you work.

Make the Dough: In a small bowl, whisk together the
flour, ginger, cinnamon, baking soda, salt, cloves, allspice,
and nutmeg. Set aside.

In a large mixing bowl, beat the butter and brown sugar on
medium speed until light and fluffy. Add the molasses and
milk and beat until smooth. Add the flour mixture and beat
until no dry streaks remain. Gather the dough, then divide
in half. Roll each half into a ball, wrap tightly in plastic, then
flatten slightly to make a disc shape and refrigerate for at
least 2 hours. Dough can keep in the fridge for up to 1 week.

Bake the Cookies: Preheat the oven to 350°F (177°C) and
line one or more baking sheets with parchment paper. Fill
a small, wide bowl with granulated sugar and fill a second
bowl with powdered sugar.

Unwrap one of the discs of dough and use a sharp knife to
divide it into 12 equal portions. Roll one of the portions into
a ball, then roll it in the granulated sugar until evenly coated.
Then roll it in the powdered sugar until evenly coated and
place it on the prepared baking sheet. Repeat with the remaining dough, leaving 2 inches of space between each one
and placing approximately 12 dough balls per sheet.

Bake for 11 to 13 minutes, until the tops are cracked and the
centers no longer appear wet. If baking two pans at once,
swap the positions of the pans halfway through to ensure
the cookies bake evenly.

Let the cookies cool on the baking sheet for 5 minutes, then
transfer to a wire rack to cool completely. Enjoy!

Makes

about 16
(4-inch)
cookies

Legit Toasted Almond Chocolate Chunk Cookies

1 cup (113 g) unsalted whole almonds

2 cups plus 2 tablespoons (255 g) all-purpose flour

½ teaspoon baking soda

1 teaspoon salt

1½ sticks (170 g) unsalted butter, at room temperature

1 cup (213 g) brown sugar

¾ cup (149 g) granulated sugar

2 large eggs, at room temperature

1 tablespoon vanilla extract

1 cup (170 g) coarsely chopped bittersweet chocolate (about 65% cacao)

Flaky sea salt, for garnish

Looking for a big cookie? This is your knight or dame in shining armor. Overflowing with toasted almonds and huge chunks of dark chocolate, our heroic and super-delicious recipe is here to save the day. With a convincingly crispy outside and a mighty chewy center, this sizable cookie earns its "legit" name, and will rescue you from your late-night munchies.

Make the Dough: Scatter the almonds in a dry skillet and place over medium heat. Cook, stirring occasionally, until toasted and fragrant, 5 to 7 minutes. Transfer to a heatproof plate and set in the freezer for 5 minutes to cool. Finely chop the almonds, then set aside.

In a small bowl, whisk together the flour, baking soda, and salt. Set aside.

In a large mixing bowl, beat the butter, brown sugar, and granulated sugar on medium speed until light and fluffy. Add the eggs and vanilla and beat until smooth. Add the flour mixture and beat until no dry streaks remain. Add the bittersweet chocolate and almonds, then stir by hand until evenly distributed in the dough. Cover the bowl with plastic and refrigerate for at least 2 hours. Dough can keep in the fridge for up to 1 week.

Bake the Cookies: Preheat the oven to 325°F (163°C) and line one or more baking sheets with parchment paper.

Scoop about ¼ cup dough but do not roll it into a ball: keep it as a rough-edged clump, then place it on the prepared baking sheet. Repeat with the remaining dough, leaving 4 inches of space between each one and placing approximately 8 dough balls per sheet.

Bake for 18 to 22 minutes, until the edges are golden and the centers no longer appear wet. If baking two pans at once, swap the positions of the pans halfway through to ensure the cookies bake evenly.

Let the cookies cool on the baking sheet for 5 minutes, then transfer to a wire rack to cool completely. Sprinkle each cookie with a pinch of sea salt. Enjoy!

No-Bake Tropical Rum Balls

22 whole graham crackers (334 g)

7 tablespoons (45 g) sweetened shredded coconut

1 cup (113 g) powdered sugar, plus more for rolling

¼ teaspoon salt

Grated zest from 1 lime

¼ cup (60 ml) silver or gold rum

¼ cup (60 ml) pineapple juice

1 teaspoon vanilla extract

Welcome to the tropics. This easy no-bake recipe is a vacation for your senses. Rum balls are typically prepared during the holidays, but our sunny version can be made anytime. Similar to a coconut daiquiri, these bite-size truffles are blended with the flavors of coconut, pineapple, lime zest, and rum. Lightly rolled in powdered sugar, this chewy, cake-like confection is paradise in a ball.

Place the graham crackers in a food processor, breaking them up with your hands. Pulse until coarsely ground, then add the coconut, powdered sugar, salt, and lime zest. Pulse until evenly blended and sandy-textured. Transfer to a medium bowl, then add the rum, pineapple juice, and vanilla and stir by hand until evenly blended. Cover the bowl and refrigerate for 20 minutes.

Line a baking sheet with parchment paper and fill a wide, shallow bowl with powdered sugar.

Scoop about 1 tablespoon dough into a ball and roll it in the bowl of powdered sugar until evenly coated in a thin layer. Place the cookie on the prepared baking sheet and repeat with the remaining dough. Keep in a covered container at room temperature for up to a week. Enjoy!

1 large egg, at room temperature

¾ cup plus 1 tablespoon
(174 g) brown sugar

¾ cup plus 2 tablespoons (225 g)
no-stir creamy peanut butter

¼ teaspoon vanilla extract

20 to 22 chocolate kisses

5-Ingredient Peanut Butter Blossoms

Introducing your new favorite five-ingredient cookie. Simply made with peanut butter, brown sugar, vanilla, and an egg, these effortless treats are crowned with a chocolate kiss. Serve them warm for an indulgent and unforgettable melt-in-your-mouth experience, or wait (if you have the willpower) as they cool into a soft and chewy cookie that blossoms with chocolate peanut butter deliciousness.

Make the Dough: In a large mixing bowl, beat the egg and brown sugar on medium speed until blended. Add the peanut butter and vanilla and beat until smooth. Cover the bowl with plastic and refrigerate for at least 2 hours. Dough can keep in the fridge for up to 1 week.

Bake the Cookies: Preheat the oven to 350°F (177°C) and line one or more baking sheets with parchment paper.

Scoop about 1 tablespoon dough into a ball and place it on the prepared baking sheet. Repeat with the remaining dough, leaving 2 inches of space between each one and placing approximately 12 dough balls per sheet. Place the baking sheets in the freezer for 15 minutes; this helps the cookies keep their shape while baking.

Transfer the baking sheets directly to the oven and bake for 11 to 13 minutes, until the edges are golden. If baking two pans at once, swap the positions of the pans halfway through to ensure the cookies bake evenly.

As soon as the cookies come out of the oven, gently press a chocolate kiss into the center of each one. Let the cookies cool on the baking sheet for 5 minutes, then transfer to a wire rack to cool completely. Enjoy!

Amaretto-Glazed Oatmeal Brown Sugar Cookies

For the Cookies

1 cup (89 g) rolled oats

1 cup (120 g) all-purpose flour

1 teaspoon ground cinnamon

½ teaspoon salt

¼ teaspoon baking powder

¼ teaspoon baking soda

¼ teaspoon ground nutmeg

1 stick (113 g) unsalted butter, at room temperature

¾ cup (160 g) brown sugar

1 large egg, at room temperature

½ teaspoon vanilla extract

For the Amaretto Glaze

1¼ cups (141 g) powdered sugar

3 tablespoons plus 1 teaspoon amaretto liqueur

Crispy, or not crispy? That is the question. If your ideal oatmeal cookie is chewy and chunky, head to page 50 in the first chapter. But if you like your oatmeal cookies a bit thinner, crispier, and minus the raisins, look no further. Dipped in a glistening, sweet amaretto glaze, these oatmeal brown sugar cookies are such stuff as dreams are made on.

Make the Dough: Place the oats in a food processor and pulse several times until coarsely chopped. Transfer to a small bowl, then add the flour, cinnamon, salt, baking powder, baking soda, and nutmeg. Whisk to combine, then set aside.

In a large mixing bowl, beat the butter and brown sugar on medium speed until light and fluffy. Add the egg and vanilla and beat until smooth. Add the flour mixture and beat until no dry streaks remain. Cover the bowl with plastic and refrigerate for at least 2 hours. Dough can keep in the fridge for up to 1 week.

Bake the Cookies: Preheat the oven to 350°F (177°C) and line one or more baking sheets with parchment paper.

Scoop 1½ tablespoons dough into a ball and place it on the prepared baking sheet. Repeat with the remaining dough, leaving 2 inches of space between each one and placing approximately 12 dough balls per sheet.

Bake for 11 to 13 minutes, until the edges of the cookies begin to darken slightly and the centers no longer appear wet. If baking two pans at once, swap the positions of the pans halfway through to ensure the cookies bake evenly.

Let the cookies cool on the baking sheet for 5 minutes, then transfer to a wire rack to cool completely.

Glaze the Cookies: In a small, wide bowl, stir together the powdered sugar and amaretto liqueur until smooth and creamy.

Hold a cookie by its edges, then dip the top of the cookie in the glaze, allowing the excess glaze to drip back into the bowl. Return the cookie to the rack to dry, and repeat with the remaining cookies. The glazed cookies will dry in about 20 minutes. Enjoy!

chapter 3

frosted and filled

Frosted and filled, and dressed to impress, these showstoppers will surely Take the Cookie at any celebration. Our Soft and Chewy Carrot Cake Cookies (page 90) are bound to turn heads when you surprise your company with a platter of these golden treats, and you can confidently mic-drop after setting a tray of Gingerbread Whoopie Pies with Vanilla Marshmallow Crème (page 106) on the table. If you really want to stir things up, our coffee-infused Iced Horchata Latte Cookies (page 92) are guaranteed to bring some pep to the party. Whether you're craving ice-cream sandwiches or linzers, shortbread or biscotti, this chapter is loaded with all things frosted and filled.

Chocolate Hazelnut Linzer Cookies

We interrupt this program to bring you something scrumptious. Tonight's forecast calls for a baking storm with 100 percent chance of cookies. With a light and crumbly texture that's similar to shortbread, these tender linzers are infused with the warm, rich flavor of toasted hazelnuts. In the center lies a silky chocolate hazelnut filling, and the secret to this magical middle is a splash of Frangelico, a hazelnut liqueur with delicate hints of vanilla and cocoa. Lightly dusted with a snowfall of powdered sugar, they feature star-shaped cutouts to reveal the chocolate within. We urge you to stay indoors and bake these cozy cookies tonight.

For the Cookies

¾ cup (90 g) raw unsalted hazelnuts

2¼ cups (270 g) all-purpose flour

½ teaspoon salt

¼ teaspoon ground cinnamon

2 sticks (226 g) unsalted butter, at room temperature

⅔ cup (132 g) granulated sugar

1 large egg, at room temperature

1 teaspoon vanilla extract

Powdered sugar, for dusting

For the Chocolate Hazelnut Filling

6 tablespoons (110 g) Nutella or other chocolate-hazelnut spread

3 teaspoons heavy cream

1½ teaspoons Frangelico or another hazelnut liqueur

Make the Dough: Scatter the hazelnuts in a dry skillet and place over medium heat. Cook, stirring occasionally, until toasted and fragrant, 5 to 7 minutes. Transfer to a heatproof plate and set in the freezer for 5 minutes to cool. Remove any loose, papery skins, then transfer the nuts to a food processor. Pulse until finely ground and sandy-textured, then set aside.

In a small bowl, whisk together the flour, salt, and cinnamon. Add the hazelnuts and whisk to combine. Set aside.

In a large mixing bowl, beat the butter and granulated sugar on medium speed until light and fluffy. Add the egg and vanilla and beat until smooth. Add the flour mixture and beat until no dry streaks remain. Gather the dough into a ball, then flatten slightly to make a disc shape, wrap tightly in plastic, and refrigerate for at least 2 hours. Dough can keep in the fridge for up to 1 week.

Bake the Cookies: Preheat the oven to 350°F (177°C) and line one or more baking sheets with parchment paper.

Unwrap the disc of dough and place it on a lightly floured work surface. Roll the dough to a large circle about ⅛ inch thick. The dough may crack slightly, so if this happens, gently press it back together as you roll. Using a 2½-inch ruffled circle cutter, cut out as many circles as possible from the dough. Then, using a 1-inch star cutter, cut out the centers of half of the cookies. Transfer all the cookies to the prepared baking sheets, leaving about 1 inch of space between each cookie. Gather and reroll the dough scraps, then cut out the remaining cookies. Place the baking sheets in the freezer for 15 minutes; this helps the cookies keep their shape while baking.

Transfer the baking sheets directly to the oven and bake for 12 to 14 minutes, until the edges of the cookies are lightly golden. If baking two pans at once, swap the positions of the pans halfway through to ensure the cookies bake evenly.

Let the cookies cool on the baking sheet for 5 minutes, then transfer to a wire rack to cool completely.

Make the Filling and Assemble the Cookies: In a small bowl, stir together the Nutella, heavy cream, and Frangelico until smooth and creamy. Set aside.

Separate the two cookie shapes—the whole circles will be the base for the sandwiches, and the star cutouts will be the tops. Dust the star cutout cookies with powdered sugar. Set aside.

Arrange the cookie bases with the flat side up. Spread about 2 teaspoons filling over each cookie in a smooth layer. Place the sugar-dusted cookie tops on each base to make a sandwich. Enjoy!

Note: If a 1-inch star cutter is unavailable, any 1-inch shape will work.

Brown Butter Pecan Cookies with Salted Caramel Filling

For the Cookies

2 sticks (226 g) unsalted butter

¾ cup (85 g) pecans

2¼ cups (270 g) all-purpose flour

½ teaspoon baking powder

½ teaspoon salt

¾ cup (149 g) granulated sugar

1 large egg, at room temperature

1 teaspoon vanilla extract

For the Salted Caramel Filling

½ cup (99 g) granulated sugar

1 tablespoon plus 1 teaspoon water

1 tablespoon light corn syrup

¼ cup (59 ml) heavy cream

1 tablespoon unsalted butter

½ teaspoon salt

½ teaspoon vanilla extract

Hurry, hurry, step right up! This astounding cookie is a carnival of flavor. You'll marvel at the rich and creamy salted caramel filling, which is nestled between two perfectly crisp cookies made with brown butter, vanilla, and toasted pecans. Entertaining—and appetizing—for the whole family, get ready for the culinary ride of your life.

Make the Dough: Place the 2 sticks butter in a small saucepan and set over medium-low heat. Melt the butter, stirring often, then continue stirring as the butter becomes foamy and the solids at the bottom of the pan begin to turn golden brown. When the butter solids are dark brown—but not burned—immediately remove the pan from the heat and pour the butter into a small heatproof bowl to stop the cooking process. Let the butter cool to room temperature, 30 to 45 minutes.

Scatter the pecans in a dry skillet and place over medium heat. Cook, stirring occasionally, until toasted and fragrant, 5 to 7 minutes. Transfer to a heatproof plate and set in the freezer for 5 minutes to cool. Finely chop the pecans, then set aside.

In a small bowl, whisk together the flour, baking powder, and ½ teaspoon salt. Set aside.

In a large mixing bowl, beat the brown butter and ¾ cup sugar on medium speed until blended. Add the egg and 1 teaspoon vanilla and beat until smooth. Add the flour mixture and beat until no dry streaks remain. Add the pecans, then stir by hand until evenly distributed in the dough. Gather the dough into a ball, then flatten slightly to make a disc shape, wrap tightly in plastic, and refrigerate for at least 2 hours. Dough can keep in the fridge for up to 1 week.

Continued...

Make the Filling: In a small saucepan, combine the ½ cup sugar, water, and corn syrup. Set over medium heat and cook, stirring often, until amber-colored, 8 to 10 minutes. Remove from the heat and add the heavy cream, 1 tablespoon butter, ½ teaspoon salt, and ½ teaspoon vanilla. Stir until smooth and blended, then transfer to a heatproof sealed container in the fridge to cool. The caramel will stay fresh for up to a week in the fridge—note that the caramel thickens when refrigerated, so it must be brought to room temperature for a spreadable consistency before use.

Bake the Cookies: Preheat the oven to 350°F (177°C) and line one or more baking sheets with parchment paper.

Unwrap the disc of dough and place it on a lightly floured work surface. Roll the dough to a large circle about ⅛ inch thick. The dough may crack slightly, so if this happens, gently press it back together as you roll. Using a 2-inch circle cutter, cut out as many circles as possible from the dough. Transfer to the prepared baking sheets, leaving about 1 inch of space between each cookie. Gather and reroll the dough scraps, then cut out the remaining cookies. Place the baking sheets in the freezer for 15 minutes; this helps the cookies keep their shape while baking.

Transfer the baking sheets directly to the oven and bake for 10 to 12 minutes, until the edges of the cookies are lightly golden. If baking two pans at once, swap the positions of the pans halfway through to ensure the cookies bake evenly.

Let the cookies cool on the baking sheet for 5 minutes, then transfer to a wire rack to cool completely.

Assemble the Cookies: Arrange half of the cookies with the flat side up. Spread about 1 teaspoon of caramel over each cookie in a smooth layer. Place a second cookie on top to make a sandwich. Repeat with the remaining cookies, and enjoy!

Citrus Shortbread Cookies with Marzipan Filling

For the Cookies

2 sticks (226 g) unsalted butter, at room temperature

½ cup (99 g) granulated sugar

½ teaspoon salt

Grated zest from 1 lemon

Grated zest from 1 lime

1 teaspoon vanilla extract

2 cups (240 g) all-purpose flour

For the Marzipan

1 cup plus 3 tablespoons (110 g) almond flour

½ cup plus 2 tablespoons (70 g) powdered sugar

3 tablespoons plus 2 teaspoons granulated sugar

2 tablespoons light corn syrup

1½ teaspoons almond extract

This is pure sunshine in a cookie. Guaranteed to brighten your day, these shortbread sandwich squares are beaming with flavor. The soft and crumbly shortbread is baked with freshly grated lemon and lime zest, then filled with a generous layer of homemade marzipan. The citrus soirée is about to begin, so open your windows, little darlins', here comes the sun.

Make the Dough: In a large mixing bowl, beat the butter, ½ cup granulated sugar, and salt on medium speed until light and fluffy. Add the lemon zest, lime zest, and vanilla and beat until smooth. Add the flour and beat until no dry streaks remain. Gather the dough into a ball, then flatten slightly to make a disc shape. Wrap tightly in plastic and refrigerate for at least 2 hours. Dough can keep in the fridge for up to 1 week.

Make the Marzipan: In a food processor, combine the almond flour, powdered sugar, and 3 tablespoons plus 2 teaspoons granulated sugar and pulse until evenly blended. Add the corn syrup and almond extract and pulse until the mixture begins to clump together. To reach a spreadable consistency, add water a teaspoon at a time, as needed, up to a total of 2 tablespoons. Transfer the marzipan to a small bowl, then cover and refrigerate. The marzipan will stay fresh for up to a week in the fridge—note that the marzipan thickens when refrigerated, so it must be brought to room temperature for a spreadable consistency before use.

Bake the Cookies: Preheat the oven to 350°F (177°C) and line one or more baking sheets with parchment paper.

Unwrap the disc of dough and place it on a lightly floured work surface. Roll the dough to a large circle about ¼ inch

Continued . . .

thick. The dough may crack slightly, so if this happens, gently press it back together as you roll. Using a 2½-inch ruffled square cutter, cut out as many shapes as possible from the dough. Transfer the cookie shapes to the prepared baking sheets, leaving about 1 inch of space between each cookie. Gather and reroll the dough scraps, then cut out the remaining cookies. Place the baking sheets in the freezer for 15 minutes; this helps the cookies keep their shape while baking.

Transfer the baking sheets directly to the oven and bake for 10 to 12 minutes, until the edges of the cookies are lightly golden and the centers no longer appear wet. If baking two pans at once, swap the positions of the pans halfway through to ensure the cookies bake evenly.

Let the cookies cool on the baking sheet for 5 minutes, then transfer to a wire rack to cool completely.

Assemble the Cookies: Arrange half the cookies with the flat side up. Spread about 2 teaspoons of marzipan over each one in a smooth layer. Place a second cookie on top to make a sandwich. Repeat with the remaining cookies, and enjoy!

Note: If desired, use store-bought marzipan to save time.

Makes 20 to 22 (2½-inch) cookies

Soft and Chewy Carrot Cake Cookies

Yep, you read that right. Your favorite cake is now a cookie! Now you can have your cake and eat your cookie too. You're welcome.

For the Cookies

1¾ cups (210 g) all-purpose flour

1 teaspoon ground cinnamon

½ teaspoon ground nutmeg

½ teaspoon salt

½ teaspoon cream of tartar

¼ teaspoon baking soda

¼ teaspoon ground allspice

⅛ teaspoon ground cloves

1 stick (113 g) unsalted butter, at room temperature

½ cup (107 g) brown sugar

½ cup (99 g) granulated sugar

1 large egg, at room temperature

1 teaspoon vanilla extract

¾ cup (75 g) grated carrots (1 to 2 medium)

For the Cream Cheese Frosting

6 ounces (170 g) cream cheese, at room temperature

3 tablespoons unsalted butter, at room temperature

1½ teaspoons vanilla extract

¼ teaspoon salt

1½ cups (170 g) powdered sugar

Make the Dough: In a small bowl, whisk together the flour, cinnamon, nutmeg, ½ teaspoon salt, cream of tartar, baking soda, allspice, and cloves. Set aside.

In a large mixing bowl, beat the 1 stick butter, brown sugar, and granulated sugar on medium speed until light and fluffy. Add the egg and 1 teaspoon vanilla and beat until smooth. Then add the carrots and beat until evenly combined. Add the flour mixture and beat until no dry streaks remain. Cover the bowl with plastic and refrigerate for at least 2 hours. Dough can keep in the fridge for up to 1 week.

Bake the Cookies: Preheat the oven to 350°F (177°C) and line one or more baking sheets with parchment paper.

Scoop about 1½ tablespoons dough into a ball and place it on the prepared baking sheet. Repeat with the remaining dough, leaving 2 inches of space between each one.

Bake for 12 to 14 minutes, until the edges are lightly golden and the centers no longer appear wet. If baking two pans at once, swap the positions of the pans halfway through to ensure the cookies bake evenly. As soon as the pans come out of the oven, use a wide spatula to gently press down and slightly flatten the cookies.

Let the cookies cool on the baking sheet for 5 minutes, then transfer to a wire rack to cool completely.

Make the Frosting and Assemble the Cookies: In a large mixing bowl, beat the cream cheese and 3 tablespoons butter on medium speed until light and fluffy. Add the 1½ teaspoons vanilla and ¼ teaspoon salt and beat until smooth. Sift the powdered sugar into the bowl, then continue beating until smooth and creamy.

Spread 2 teaspoons of frosting on each cookie, and enjoy!

Iced Horchata Latte Cookies

Need a little pick-me-up? Our tempting treats are just begging you to pick them up! We created a compelling cookie that tastes just like a cup of coffee. Buzzing with espresso flavor, these energetic cookies are topped with a smooth horchata-inspired icing with hints of cinnamon, almond, and vanilla, just like the refreshing Mexican *agua fresca*. The next time you're feeling hungry, tired, or thirsty, this recipe will fix all three.

For the Cookies

1½ cups (180 g) all-purpose flour

¾ teaspoon baking powder

¼ teaspoon salt

1 stick (113 g) unsalted butter, at room temperature

½ cup (57 g) powdered sugar

¼ cup (50 g) granulated sugar

1 large egg, at room temperature

2 teaspoons instant espresso powder

1 teaspoon vanilla extract

For the Horchata Icing

1 stick (113 g) unsalted butter, at room temperature

1½ teaspoons ground cinnamon

½ teaspoon vanilla extract

¼ teaspoon salt

⅛ teaspoon almond extract

1½ cups (170 g) powdered sugar

Make the Dough: In a small bowl, whisk together the flour, baking powder, and ¼ teaspoon salt. Set aside.

In a large mixing bowl, beat the 1 stick butter, powdered sugar, and granulated sugar on medium speed until light and fluffy. Add the egg, espresso powder, and 1 teaspoon vanilla and beat until smooth. Add the flour mixture and beat until no dry streaks remain. Cover the bowl with plastic and refrigerate for at least 2 hours. Dough can keep in the fridge for up to 1 week.

Bake the Cookies: Preheat the oven to 350°F (177°C) and line one or more baking sheets with parchment paper.

Scoop about 1 tablespoon dough into a ball and place it on the prepared baking sheet. Repeat with the remaining dough, leaving 2 inches of space between each one.

Bake for 12 to 14 minutes, until the edges are lightly golden and the centers no longer appear wet. If baking two pans at once, swap the positions of the pans halfway through to ensure the cookies bake evenly. As soon as the pans come out of the oven, use a wide spatula to gently press down and slightly flatten the cookies.

Let the cookies cool on the baking sheet for 5 minutes, then transfer to a wire rack to cool completely.

Make the Icing and Assemble the Cookies: In a large mixing bowl, beat the 1 stick butter on medium speed

until light and fluffy. Add the cinnamon, ½ teaspoon vanilla, ¼ teaspoon salt, and almond extract and beat until smooth. Sift the powdered sugar into the bowl, then continue beating until smooth and creamy.

Spread about 2 teaspoons of icing on top of each cookie, and enjoy!

Makes
14 to 16
(2½-inch)
cookie
sandwiches

Peach Melba Shortbread Stacks

For the Cookies

¾ cup (22 g) whole, freeze-dried raspberries

2 sticks (226 g) unsalted butter, at room temperature

½ cup (99 g) granulated sugar

1 teaspoon vanilla extract

½ teaspoon salt

2 cups (240 g) all-purpose flour

For the Peach Curd

2 small peaches (about 130 g each)

2 large egg yolks

¼ cup (50 g) granulated sugar

½ to 1 tablespoon lemon juice

Generous pinch of salt

4 tablespoons (57 g) unsalted butter, cubed

1 teaspoon vanilla extract

Looking for a summer-inspired sweet that can be made all year? You've turned to the right page. Peach Melba is a classic dessert that we've reconstructed into a cute cookie sandwich. Thin and crisp, these ruby-red raspberry ruffled cookies are bright and tangy. Filled with a sweet peach curd made with fresh peaches and vanilla, this recipe is delightful on its own, but let us remind you that classic Peach Melba is traditionally served with a scoop of vanilla ice cream. You know what to do.

Make the Dough: Place the raspberries in a food processor and pulse until finely ground into a powder. Set a fine-mesh strainer over a bowl and sift the powdered raspberries into the bowl, removing and discarding the seeds. Set aside.

In a large mixing bowl, beat the 2 sticks butter and ½ cup sugar on medium speed until light and fluffy. Add the 1 teaspoon vanilla, ½ teaspoon salt, and raspberry powder and beat until smooth. Add the flour and beat until no dry streaks remain. Gather the dough into a ball, then flatten slightly to make a disc shape, wrap tightly in plastic, and refrigerate for at least 2 hours. Dough can keep in the fridge for up to 1 week.

Make the Peach Curd: Cut the peaches in half, remove and discard the pits, and place the peach halves in a blender or food processor. Blend until smooth, and set aside.

Fill a small saucepan with 1 to 2 inches of water and bring to a simmer over medium heat. Place a medium heatproof bowl over the pan, so the bottom of the bowl rests above the surface of the simmering water. Add the peach puree, egg yolks, the ¼ cup sugar, ½ tablespoon lemon juice, and a pinch of salt and stir to combine. Continue to cook, stirring occasionally, until the curd has thickened, and the temperature reaches 170°F (77°C) on a cooking thermometer, 15 to 20 minutes. Remove from heat and add the 4 tablespoons

Continued . . .

butter and 1 teaspoon vanilla, stirring until the butter melts and the mixture is smooth and blended. Taste for lemon and add more, if needed.

Set a fine-mesh strainer over a medium heatproof bowl and strain the curd into the bowl, removing and discarding any pulp. Cover the bowl with plastic, pressing the wrap directly onto the surface of the curd to prevent a skin from forming, and refrigerate until cool, at least 2 hours. Curd can keep in the fridge for up to 1 week.

Bake the Cookies: Preheat the oven to 350°F (177°C) and line one or more baking sheets with parchment paper.

Unwrap the disc of dough and place it on a lightly floured work surface. Roll the dough to a large circle about ⅛ inch thick. The dough may crack slightly, so if this happens, gently press it back together as you roll. Using a 2½-inch ruffled square cutter, cut out as many squares as possible from the dough. Then, using a 1-inch square cutter, cut out the centers of half of the cookies. Transfer all the cookie shapes to the prepared baking sheets, leaving about 1 inch of space between each cookie. Gather and reroll the dough scraps, then cut out the remaining cookies. Place the baking sheets in the freezer for 15 minutes; this helps the cookies keep their shape while baking.

Transfer the baking sheets directly to the oven and bake for 10 to 12 minutes, until the edges of the cookies are lightly golden. If baking two pans at once, swap the positions of the pans halfway through to ensure the cookies bake evenly.

Let the cookies cool on the baking sheet for 5 minutes, then transfer to a wire rack to cool completely.

Assemble the Cookies: Separate the two cookie shapes— the whole squares will be the base for the sandwiches and the square cutouts will be the tops.

Arrange the cookie bases with the flat side up. Spread about 2 teaspoons of peach curd over each cookie in a smooth layer. Place the cookie tops on each base to make a sandwich. Enjoy!

For the Cookies

2 cups (473 ml) unfiltered
apple juice

3 cups (360 g) all-purpose flour

1 teaspoon baking soda

1 teaspoon cream of tartar

1 teaspoon ground cinnamon

¼ teaspoon ground nutmeg

¼ teaspoon salt

⅛ teaspoon ground cloves

1½ sticks (170 g) unsalted butter,
at room temperature

¾ cup (149 g) granulated sugar

¾ cup (160 g) brown sugar

1 large egg, at room temperature

½ cup (80 g) peeled and grated
Granny Smith apples (about a
½ apple)

For the Cinnamon Frosting

1 stick (113 g) unsalted butter,
at room temperature

2¼ teaspoons ground cinnamon,
plus more for garnish

½ teaspoon vanilla extract

¼ teaspoon salt

1½ cups (170 g) powdered sugar

Cinnamon-Frosted Apple Cider Cookies

What's more comforting than a slice of apple pie? An apple cider cookie full of the flavors of fall! Baked with cinnamon, nutmeg, cloves, and freshly grated Granny Smiths, these autumnal cookies are soft and moist with a gooey, pie-like center. Topped with a swirl of cinnamon frosting—and served à la mode if you're feeling fancy—put on a cozy sweater and prepare your palate for an intense apple experience you'll never forget.

Make the Dough: Pour the apple juice into a small saucepan and bring to a simmer over medium heat. Reduce the heat to medium-low and continue to simmer, stirring occasionally, until the juice reduces to about ¼ cup of thick, amber-colored syrup, 20 to 30 minutes. Transfer to a heat-proof bowl and refrigerate until cooled to room temperature, 10 to 15 minutes.

In a small bowl, whisk together the flour, baking soda, cream of tartar, 1 teaspoon cinnamon, nutmeg, ¼ teaspoon salt, and cloves. Set aside.

In a large mixing bowl, beat the 1½ sticks butter, granulated sugar, and brown sugar on medium speed until light and fluffy. Add the egg, grated apple, and the apple syrup and beat until smooth. Add the flour mixture and beat until no dry streaks remain. Cover the bowl with plastic and refrigerate for at least 2 hours. Dough can keep in the fridge for up to 1 week.

Bake the Cookies: Preheat the oven to 350°F (177°C) and line one or more baking sheets with parchment paper.

Scoop about 1½ tablespoons dough into a ball and place it on the prepared baking sheet. Repeat with the remaining dough, leaving 2 inches of space between each one.

Bake for 11 to 13 minutes, until the edges are lightly golden and the centers no longer appear wet. If baking two pans at

Continued...

once, swap the positions of the pans halfway through to ensure the cookies bake evenly.

Let the cookies cool on the baking sheet for 5 minutes, then transfer to a wire rack to cool completely.

Make the Frosting and Assemble the Cookies: In a large mixing bowl, beat the 1 stick butter on medium speed until light and fluffy. Add the 2¼ teaspoons cinnamon, vanilla, and ¼ teaspoon salt and beat until smooth. Sift the powdered sugar into the bowl, then continue beating until smooth and creamy.

Spread about 1½ teaspoons icing on top of each cookie, then garnish with a pinch of cinnamon, and enjoy!

For the Peppermint Chip Ice Cream

1 (14-ounce/396 g) can sweetened condensed milk

1 tablespoon powdered sugar

1 teaspoon peppermint extract

¼ teaspoon vanilla extract

⅛ teaspoon salt

2 cups (473 ml) heavy cream

½ cup (90 g) mini semisweet chocolate chips, plus more for garnish

For the Cookies

1 cup (170 g) bittersweet chocolate chips (about 65% cacao)

⅓ cup (57 g) chopped unsweetened chocolate (100% cacao)

1 stick (113 g) unsalted butter, cubed

2 teaspoons instant coffee crystals

1 cup (120 g) all-purpose flour

1 teaspoon baking powder

1 teaspoon salt

1½ cups (297 g) granulated sugar

4 large eggs, at room temperature

2 teaspoons vanilla extract

1 cup (170 g) semisweet chocolate chips (about 45% cacao)

Peppermint Mocha Ice-Cream Sandwiches

It would be sacrilege if we didn't include an ice-cream-filled recipe in this chapter. Rich and chocolaty, these triple chocolate mocha cookies are sandwiched with an ultrasimple, no-churn peppermint chip ice cream. The cookies are dark and fudgy, and the minty ice cream is easy to whip up—no machine required! It's creamy like gelato and loaded with mini chocolate chips in every bite. These cool cookie sandwiches are the perfect way to eat ice cream all year round.

Make the Ice Cream: Place an empty loaf pan (about 9 x 5 inches) in the freezer to chill while preparing the ice cream.

In a food processor or blender, combine the condensed milk, powdered sugar, peppermint extract, ¼ teaspoon vanilla, and ⅛ teaspoon salt. Blend until smooth and creamy, then transfer to a medium bowl and set aside.

Pour the heavy cream into a large, clean mixing bowl, and use an electric mixer on medium speed to whip the cream until it holds firm peaks when the beaters are lifted, 2 to 3 minutes.

Scoop about 1 cup whipped cream and add it to the peppermint mixture, stirring until no streaks remain. Then pour the peppermint-cream mixture into the large bowl of remaining whipped cream and stir gently by hand until nearly all the streaks are gone. Add the mini chips, and without overmixing, continue stirring gently until no streaks remain. Pour the mixture into the loaf pan and smooth the top evenly. Sprinkle with additional mini chips for garnish, then cover the pan and place in the freezer for at least 4 hours. Ice cream can keep in the freezer for up to 1 month.

Make the Dough: Fill a small saucepan with 1 to 2 inches of water, and bring to a simmer over medium heat. Place a small heatproof bowl over the pan, so the bottom of the

Continued . . .

Note: If you would like your ice cream to be a minty shade of green, add 2 to 3 drops green food coloring or ¼ teaspoon powdered spirulina.

bowl rests above the surface of the simmering water. Place the bittersweet chips, unsweetened chocolate, butter, and coffee crystals in the bowl, and stir until melted and smooth with no lumps remaining. Carefully remove the hot bowl from the pan and set aside to cool for 5 to 10 minutes.

In a small bowl, whisk together the flour, baking powder, and 1 teaspoon salt. Set aside.

In a large mixing bowl, beat the sugar and eggs on medium speed until light and foamy, 2 to 3 minutes. Add the 2 teaspoons vanilla and melted chocolate and beat until smooth. Add the flour mixture and beat until no dry streaks remain. Add the semisweet chocolate chips, then stir by hand until evenly distributed in the dough. Cover the bowl with plastic and refrigerate for at least 2 hours. Dough can keep in the fridge for up to 1 week.

Bake the Cookies: Preheat the oven to 350°F (177°C) and line one or more baking sheets with parchment paper.

Scoop about 2 tablespoons dough into a ball and place it on the prepared baking sheet. Repeat with the remaining dough, leaving 2 inches of space between each one.

Bake for 10 to 13 minutes, until the edges are set but the centers still appear wet. If baking two pans at once, swap the positions of the pans halfway through to ensure the cookies bake evenly. As soon as the pans come out of the oven, use a wide spatula to gently press down and slightly flatten the cookies.

Let the cookies cool on the baking sheet for 5 minutes, then transfer to a wire rack for 15 minutes to cool completely. Once cool, transfer the cookies to a sealed container in the fridge and refrigerate for at least 2 hours. Cookies can keep in the fridge for up to 1 week.

Assemble the Cookies: Place one cookie flat side up on a plate, then top with a generous scoop of peppermint chip ice cream. Place a second cookie on top to make a sandwich, then gently press them together. Set the ice-cream sandwich on a plate in the freezer to stay cold while you prepare the remaining sandwiches. Keep frozen until ready to serve, and enjoy!

Lemon Tart Linzer Cookies

These mouthwatering linzers are not for the faint of heart: please proceed with cookie caution. If you like sweet and chocolaty linzer cookies, turn to page 82, but if you're a fan of tart and lemony desserts, you've just discovered your sour soulmate. In these delectable delights, two buttery cookies baked with a hint of lemon zest, cinnamon, and vanilla are layered with a tangy lemon curd that's guaranteed to tingle your taste buds. Lemon lovers, rejoice!

For the Cookies

2¼ cups (270 g) all-purpose flour

1 cup (93 g) almond flour

½ teaspoon salt

⅛ teaspoon ground cinnamon

2 sticks (226 g) unsalted butter, at room temperature

⅔ cup (132 g) granulated sugar

Grated zest from 1 lemon

1 large egg, at room temperature

1 teaspoon vanilla extract

Powdered sugar, for dusting

For the Lemon Curd

¼ cup (50 g) granulated sugar

2 large eggs

1 large egg yolk

¼ cup (60 ml) lemon juice

⅛ teaspoon salt

1 tablespoon unsalted butter, cubed

Make the Dough: In a small bowl, whisk together the all-purpose flour, almond flour, ½ teaspoon salt, and cinnamon. Set aside.

In a large mixing bowl, beat the 2 sticks butter and ⅔ cup sugar on medium speed until blended. Add the lemon zest, 1 egg, and vanilla and beat until smooth. Add the flour mixture and beat until no dry streaks remain. Gather the dough into a ball, then flatten slightly to make a disc shape, wrap tightly in plastic, and refrigerate for at least 2 hours. Dough can keep in the fridge for up to 1 week.

Make the Lemon Curd: Fill a small saucepan with 1 to 2 inches of water, and bring to a simmer over medium heat. Place a medium heatproof bowl over the pan, so the bottom of the bowl rests above the surface of the simmering water. Add the ¼ cup sugar, 2 eggs, 1 egg yolk, lemon juice, and ⅛ teaspoon salt and stir to combine. Continue to cook, stirring occasionally, until the curd has thickened and the temperature reaches 170°F (77°C) on a cooking thermometer, 15 to 20 minutes. Remove from the heat and add the 1 tablespoon butter, stirring until the butter melts and the mixture is smooth and blended.

Set a fine-mesh strainer over a medium heatproof bowl and strain the curd into the bowl, removing and discarding any solids. Cover the bowl with plastic, pressing the wrap

Continued ...

directly onto the surface of the curd to prevent a skin from forming, and refrigerate until cool, at least 2 hours. Curd can keep in the fridge for up to 1 week.

Bake the Cookies: Preheat the oven to 350°F (177°C) and line one or more baking sheets with parchment paper.

Unwrap the disc of dough and place it on a lightly floured work surface. Roll the dough to a large circle about ⅛ inch thick. The dough may crack slightly, so if this happens, gently press it back together as you roll. Using a 2½-inch ruffled circle cutter, cut out as many circles as possible from the dough. Then, using a 1-inch ruffled circle cutter, cut out off-center holes in half the cookies. Transfer all the cookie shapes to the prepared baking sheets, leaving about 1 inch of space between each cookie. Gather and reroll the dough scraps, then cut out the remaining cookies. Place the baking sheets in the freezer for 15 minutes; this helps the cookies keep their shape while baking.

Transfer the baking sheets directly to the oven and bake for 12 to 14 minutes, until the edges of the cookies are lightly golden. If baking two pans at once, swap the positions of the pans halfway through to ensure the cookies bake evenly.

Let the cookies cool on the baking sheet for 5 minutes, then transfer to a wire rack to cool completely.

Assemble the Cookies: Separate the two cookie shapes—the whole circles will be the base for the sandwiches and the circle cutouts will be the tops. Dust the cutout cookies with powdered sugar and set aside.

Arrange the cookie bases with the flat side up. Spread about 2 teaspoons lemon curd over each cookie in a smooth layer. Place the sugar-dusted cookie tops on each base to make a sandwich. Enjoy!

Gingerbread Whoopie Pies with Vanilla Marshmallow Crème

For the Cookies

2¼ cups (270 g) all-purpose flour

1 tablespoon ground ginger

2¼ teaspoons ground cinnamon

1¼ teaspoons baking soda

½ teaspoon baking powder

½ teaspoon salt

½ teaspoon ground cloves

½ teaspoon ground allspice

¼ teaspoon ground nutmeg

1 stick (113 g) unsalted butter, at room temperature

1 cup (213 g) brown sugar

1 large egg, at room temperature

1 teaspoon vanilla extract

¼ cup (85 g) molasses

¾ cup (177 ml) buttermilk

For the Vanilla Marshmallow Crème

2 sticks (226 g) unsalted butter, at room temperature

1 cup (113 g) powdered sugar, sifted

1 (7-ounce/198 g) jar marshmallow crème

1 tablespoon vanilla extract

¼ teaspoon salt

All we want for Christmas are these silky whoopie pies. Two soft, cake-like gingerbread cookies are sandwiched together with a smooth vanilla marshmallow crème—it's like taking a bite out of a gingerbread cloud. Filled with the classic flavors of ginger, cloves, allspice, and molasses, you'll want to deck your halls year-round with these heavenly handheld treats.

Make the Dough: In a small bowl, whisk together the flour, ginger, cinnamon, baking soda, baking powder, ½ teaspoon salt, cloves, allspice, and nutmeg. Set aside.

In a large mixing bowl, beat the 1 stick butter and brown sugar on medium speed until light and fluffy. Add the egg and 1 teaspoon vanilla and beat until smooth. Then add the molasses and beat until combined. Add the buttermilk and beat until evenly blended. Then add the flour mixture and beat until no dry streaks remain—note that the dough may appear to separate at first, but continue beating and it will blend evenly. Cover the bowl with plastic and refrigerate for at least 2 hours. Dough can keep in the fridge for up to 1 week.

Bake the Cookies: Preheat the oven to 350°F (177°C) and line one or more baking sheets with parchment paper.

Scoop about 2 tablespoons dough into a ball and place it on the prepared baking sheet. Repeat with the remaining dough, leaving 2 inches of space between each one.

Bake for 10 to 12 minutes, until the edges have darkened slightly and the centers no longer appear wet. If baking two pans at once, swap the positions of the pans halfway through to ensure the cookies bake evenly.

Continued . . .

Let the cookies cool on the baking sheet for 5 minutes, then transfer to a wire rack to cool completely.

Make the Marshmallow Crème and Assemble the Cookies: In a large mixing bowl, beat the 2 sticks butter and powdered sugar on medium speed until light and fluffy. Add the marshmallow crème, 1 tablespoon vanilla, and ¼ teaspoon salt and beat until smooth.

Place one of the cookies flat side up on a piece of parchment. Scoop or pipe several tablespoons of filling onto the cookie in an even layer about ½ inch thick. Top with a second cookie to make a sandwich. Repeat with the remaining cookies and filling, and enjoy!

For the Cookies

2 cups (240 g) all-purpose flour

1½ teaspoons baking powder

½ teaspoon salt

¼ teaspoon ground cinnamon

6 tablespoons (85 g) unsalted
butter, at room temperature

1 cup (198 g) granulated sugar

2 large eggs, at room temperature

2 teaspoons vanilla extract

½ teaspoon almond extract

1 cup (140 g) raw unsalted
pistachios, coarsely chopped

For the Pomegranate Glaze

½ cup (57 g) powdered sugar

2 teaspoons pomegranate juice

1 teaspoon pomegranate molasses
(see note)

Pistachio Biscotti with Tangy Pomegranate Glaze

Wait! Before you flip past this page because of any trau-matizing past biscotti experiences, let us assure you that these are different. We, too, aren't usually fans of this of-ten stale, bland, and dry cookie, but our version is just the opposite. These twice-baked biscuits are sweet, crunchy, and filled with chopped pistachios: perfectly crispy on the outside, chewy and tender in the middle, and flavored with cinnamon, sugar, and a hint of almond extract. You haven't officially tried biscotti until you've made this per-suasively delicious recipe.

Make the Dough: In a small bowl, whisk together the flour, baking powder, salt, and cinnamon. Set aside.

In a large mixing bowl, beat the butter and sugar on medium speed until light and fluffy. Add the eggs, vanilla, and al-mond extract and beat until smooth. Add the flour mixture and beat until no dry streaks remain. Add the pistachios, then stir by hand until evenly distributed in the dough.

Bake the Cookies: Preheat the oven to 350°F (177°C) and line a baking sheet with parchment paper.

Divide the dough in half and place the two halves on the prepared baking sheet, several inches apart. Form each half into a loaf shape about 7 inches long, 4 inches wide, and 1 inch tall.

Bake for 25 to 30 minutes, until the edges are golden and the centers no longer appear wet. Let the loaves cool on the baking sheet for 10 minutes, then transfer to a cutting board and cut into 1-inch-thick slices. Arrange the slices cut side down on the baking sheet and bake for 5 minutes. Flip the slices over and bake for another 5 minutes.

Continued . . .

Let the cookies cool on the baking sheet for 5 minutes, then transfer to a wire rack to cool completely, about 30 minutes.

Make the Glaze and Assemble the Cookies: In a small bowl, stir together the powdered sugar, pomegranate juice, and pomegranate molasses until smooth and creamy, adding more juice, if needed to thin.

Arrange the biscotti right side up on the wire rack. Drizzle each one with pomegranate glaze, allowing the glaze to drip down the sides. The glazed cookies will dry in about 20 minutes. Enjoy!

Note: Pomegranate molasses is a tart, syrupy juice concentrate often used in Middle Eastern recipes. It is available in the international section of many grocery stores and online. If unavailable, it can be substituted with balsamic vinegar.

Orange Cream Rolled Wafer Cookies

Did you hear that sound? That's the satisfying crunch from our rolled wafer cookies. Not only are they ear-catching, they're delicious. Inspired by classic orange Creamsicles, our timeless treats taste just like the originals. Delicately crisp and orange-flavored on the outside, they're generously filled with a velvety vanilla cream center. One bite and you'll be transported back to your favorite childhood dessert . . . earplugs not included.

For the Cookies

1 stick (113 g) unsalted butter, at room temperature

¾ cup (149 g) granulated sugar

4 large egg whites, at room temperature

Grated zest from 2 oranges

1 teaspoon vanilla extract

⅛ teaspoon salt

¾ cup (90 g) all-purpose flour

2 to 3 drops orange food coloring (see note)

For the Vanilla Marshmallow Crème

1 stick (113 g) unsalted butter, at room temperature

½ cup (57 g) powdered sugar, sifted

¾ cup (100 g) marshmallow crème

1½ teaspoons vanilla extract

Pinch of salt

Make the Dough: In a large mixing bowl, beat the 1 stick butter and granulated sugar on medium speed until light and fluffy. Add the egg whites and beat until smooth and foamy. Then add the orange zest, 1 teaspoon vanilla, and ⅛ teaspoon salt and beat until combined. Add the flour and beat until blended. Preheat the oven to 400°F (204°C) and line a baking sheet with parchment paper.

Bake the Cookies: Scoop about ½ cup batter and place in a small bowl. Add a few drops of orange food coloring and stir to blend, adding more color if desired. Transfer the orange batter to a piping bag with a small round tip, or a zip-top bag with a corner cut off. Set aside.

Scoop ½ tablespoon untinted batter onto the prepared baking sheet and use an offset spatula to spread it into a rectangular shape about 4 x 3 inches in an even, smooth layer—note that the batter will be spread extremely thin, almost transparent. Repeat with three more scoops batter, using ½ tablespoon batter each time, spacing them evenly around the baking sheet with several inches between each rectangle. Use the piping bag to pipe parallel diagonal orange lines on each one.

Bake for 4 to 6 minutes, until the edges are golden brown. As soon as the baking sheet comes out of the oven, use a spatula to carefully peel off one of the cookies from the parchment, working quickly before it cools. Flip the cookie

Continued . . .

Note: If orange food coloring is unavailable, simply combine 1-part red color to 1-part yellow, adjusting as needed to achieve the perfect shade of orange.

over so the orange design is face down, then place a chopstick along one of the long sides of the rectangle. Roll the cookie tightly around the chopstick, then slide it off the chopstick to make a tube. Place it seam side down on a wire rack to keep it from unrolling, then repeat with the remaining rectangles before they cool and lose their flexibility. Note that since the cookies cool quickly, it is best to bake no more than four at a time. If the cookies begin to harden before you've had a chance to roll them, you may place the baking sheet back in the oven for 45 to 60 seconds to soften them again.

Make the Marshmallow Crème and Assemble the Cookies: In a large mixing bowl, beat the 1 stick butter and powdered sugar on medium speed until light and fluffy. Add the marshmallow crème, 1½ teaspoons vanilla, and a pinch of salt and beat until smooth.

Transfer a generous scoop of marshmallow crème into a piping bag fitted with a small round tip or a zip-top bag with a corner cut off. Insert the tip of the bag into one of the cookie tubes and fill it with marshmallow crème. You may need to pipe more cream into the other end of the tube to completely fill the cookie. Repeat with the remaining cookies, and enjoy!

chapter 4

cute and colorful

If you're looking for a scrumptious cookie that's also cute and colorful, you've come to the right chapter. These radiant recipes are fun to make and magically delicious. Express your love with Red Velvet Cake Valentine Cookies (page 118), follow the yellow brick road to our Chocolate Rainbow Meltaways (page 134), or summon some spooky spirits with Haunted Halloween Haystacks (page 138). There are also holiday cookies for special occasions like our festive Have Yourself a Merry Little Cookie (page 142) and Colorful Confetti Sugar Cookies (page 120) which will make all your birthday wishes come true. Decorated to the nines, these colorful confections are guaranteed to Take the Cookie. Put on an adorable apron—it's time to get cute and colorful!

20 to 22 (3-inch) cookies

2 cups (240 g) all-purpose flour

1 teaspoon baking powder

¼ teaspoon baking soda

⅓ cup (28 g) unsweetened cocoa powder

½ teaspoon salt

1 stick (113 g) unsalted butter, at room temperature

¾ cup (149 g) granulated sugar, plus more for rolling

½ cup (107 g) brown sugar

2 large eggs, at room temperature

1 tablespoon buttermilk

2 teaspoons vanilla extract

2 teaspoons red food coloring

1 teaspoon lemon juice

Powdered sugar, for rolling

Red Velvet Cake Valentine Cookies

Love (and the aroma of cookies!) is in the air. Your Valentine will fall head over heels when you present a plateful of these crimson treats. Using the traditional flavors of red velvet cake, we transformed this celebrated dessert into a dense and fudgy cookie that's soft, moist, and chocolaty. Put on your favorite album, dim the lights, and let the cookie courtship commence.

Make the Dough: In a small bowl, whisk together the flour, baking powder, baking soda, cocoa powder, and salt. Set aside.

In a large mixing bowl, beat the butter, granulated sugar, and brown sugar on medium speed until light and fluffy. Add the eggs, buttermilk, vanilla, red food coloring, and lemon juice and beat until smooth. Place a fine-mesh strainer over the bowl, then sift in the flour mixture and beat until no dry streaks remain. Cover the bowl with plastic and refrigerate for at least 2 hours. Dough can keep in the fridge for up to 1 week.

Bake the Cookies: Preheat the oven to 350°F (177°C) and line one or more baking sheets with parchment paper. Fill a small, wide bowl with granulated sugar and fill a second bowl with powdered sugar.

Scoop 1½ tablespoons dough into a ball and roll it in the granulated sugar until evenly coated. Then roll it in the powdered sugar until evenly coated and place it on the prepared baking sheet. Repeat with the remaining dough, leaving 2 inches of space between each one and placing approximately 12 dough balls per sheet.

Bake for 11 to 13 minutes, until the tops are cracked and the centers no longer appear wet. If baking two pans at once, swap the positions of the pans halfway through to ensure the cookies bake evenly.

Let the cookies cool on the baking sheet for 5 minutes, then transfer to a wire rack to cool completely. Enjoy!

2½ cups (300 g) all-purpose flour

1 teaspoon baking soda

¾ teaspoon salt

½ teaspoon baking powder

1 stick (113 g) unsalted butter,
at room temperature

1¾ cups (347 g) granulated sugar

2 large eggs, at room temperature

1 tablespoon vanilla extract

1 cup (182 g) rainbow sprinkles

Colorful Confetti Sugar Cookies

Tastefully accessorize your next party with colorful confetti cookies. Speckled with rainbow sprinkles and baked with plenty of vanilla, our thin and chewy cookies taste just like a slice of everyone's favorite birthday cake. Beautiful and delicious, these cheerful treats are the perfect way to add some pizzazz to any celebration. Let the festivities begin!

Make the Dough: In a small bowl, whisk together the flour, baking soda, salt, and baking powder. Set aside.

In a large mixing bowl, beat the butter and sugar on medium speed until light and fluffy. Add the eggs and vanilla and beat until smooth. Add the flour mixture and beat until no dry streaks remain. Add the sprinkles and beat until evenly distributed in the dough. Cover the bowl with plastic and refrigerate for at least 2 hours. Dough can keep in the fridge for up to 1 week.

Bake the Cookies: Preheat the oven to 350°F (177°C) and line one or more baking sheets with parchment paper.

Scoop about 1½ tablespoons dough into a ball and place it on the prepared baking sheet. Repeat with the remaining dough, leaving 3 inches of space between each one and placing approximately 12 dough balls per sheet. Bake until the edges are lightly golden and the centers no longer appear wet, 10 to 12 minutes. If baking two pans at once, swap the positions of the pans halfway through to ensure the cookies bake evenly.

Let the cookies cool on the baking sheet for 5 minutes, then transfer to a wire rack to cool completely. Enjoy!

Makes
35
to 40
(1½-inch)
meringue
cookies

Gluten-Free

Dairy-Free

2 large egg whites, at room temperature

¼ teaspoon cream of tartar

Pinch of salt

½ cup (99 g) granulated sugar

½ teaspoon vanilla extract

¼ teaspoon orange extract

¼ teaspoon lemon extract

1 teaspoon grated lime zest

Orange gel food coloring

Yellow gel food coloring

Green gel food coloring

Citrus Meringue Drops

That old saying should really be "a cookie a day keeps the doctor away," because these marvelous meringues are delicate, light, and airy, and provide a burst of fresh citrus. With a crisp exterior and a soft and chewy middle, our candy-like confections are individually flavored with tangy lemon, lime, and orange. Your daily dose of vitamin C never tasted so good.

Make the Meringue: In a large mixing bowl, combine the egg whites, cream of tartar, and salt and beat using the whisk attachment on medium-low speed until foamy. Raise the speed to medium-high and continue beating until soft peaks form when the whisk is lifted. With the mixer running on medium-high, slowly add the sugar about 1 tablespoon at a time, waiting about 15 seconds between each addition so the sugar can fully dissolve. Once all the sugar has been added, continue beating until stiff peaks form when the whisk is lifted, about 5 minutes. Add the vanilla and stir gently by hand to combine. Divide the meringue mixture evenly among three small bowls. To the first bowl, stir in the orange extract. To the second bowl, stir in the lemon extract. To the third bowl, stir in the lime zest.

Bake the Meringues: Preheat the oven to 200°F (93°C) and line a baking sheet with parchment paper.

Fit a piping bag with a wide star tip. Use a small, thin paintbrush to paint 3 vertical lines of orange gel food coloring down the inside of the bag, spacing them evenly apart. Then scoop the orange-flavored meringue mixture into the bag. Pipe the mixture onto the baking sheet in small, drop-shaped kisses—note that the meringues do not spread while baking, so you only need to leave about ½ inch of space between each one. Repeat with the lemon meringue mixture using a clean piping bag and draw yellow lines of color inside the bag. Then repeat with the lime meringue mixture using a clean piping bag and draw green lines of color inside the bag.

Bake the meringues for 2 hours. Then, without opening the oven door, turn off the heat. Allow the meringues to cool in the closed oven for 30 minutes. Then open the oven door a few inches and allow the meringues to finish cooling in the oven for another 30 minutes. Remove from the oven, and enjoy!

For the Cookies

1½ cups (180 g) all-purpose flour

¼ cup (21 g) unsweetened cocoa powder

¾ teaspoon baking powder

½ teaspoon instant espresso powder

¼ teaspoon salt

1 stick (113 g) unsalted butter, at room temperature

½ cup (99 g) granulated sugar

½ cup (57 g) powdered sugar

1 large egg, at room temperature

4 teaspoons Irish cream liqueur

1 teaspoon vanilla extract

For the Irish Cream Glaze

1 cup (113 g) powdered sugar

4 teaspoons heavy cream

4 teaspoons Irish cream liqueur

⅛ teaspoon salt

Green sprinkles

Luck of the Irish Cream Cookies

Bake some cookies, pick them up, and all day long you'll have good luck. These dense, brownie-like cookies are fudgy, delicious—and lucky. Made with chocolate and hints of Irish cream liqueur, they're topped with a smooth Irish cream glaze and garnished with sparkling green sprinkles. Leave the gold to the leprechauns—you'll want to find a pot of these cookies at the end of the rainbow.

Make the Dough: In a small bowl, whisk together the flour, cocoa powder, baking powder, espresso powder, and ¼ teaspoon salt. Set aside.

In a large mixing bowl, beat the butter, granulated sugar, and ½ cup powdered sugar on medium speed until light and fluffy. Add the egg, 4 teaspoons Irish cream, and vanilla and beat until smooth. Add the flour mixture and beat until no dry streaks remain. Cover the bowl with plastic and refrigerate for at least 2 hours. Dough can keep in the fridge for up to 1 week.

Bake the Cookies: Preheat the oven to 350°F (177°C) and line one or more baking sheets with parchment paper.

Scoop about 2 tablespoons dough into a ball and place it on the prepared baking sheet. Repeat with the remaining dough, leaving 2 inches of space between each one. Bake until the edges begin to darken slightly and the centers no longer appear wet, 10 to 12 minutes. If baking two pans at once, swap the positions of the pans halfway through to ensure the cookies bake evenly. As soon as the pans come out of the oven, use a wide spatula to gently press down and slightly flatten the cookies.

Let the cookies cool on the baking sheet for 5 minutes, then transfer to a wire rack to cool completely.

Make the Glaze and Assemble the Cookies: In a small bowl, stir together the 1 cup powdered sugar, heavy cream, 4 teaspoons Irish cream, and ⅛ teaspoon salt until smooth, adding more cream, if needed to thin.

Arrange the cookies on a wire rack. Using a small offset spatula, spread glaze on top of each cookie, allowing the glaze to drip down the sides. Garnish each one with green sprinkles. The glaze will dry in about 20 minutes. Enjoy!

1 cup (120 g) all-purpose flour

1 stick (113 g) unsalted butter, at room temperature

1 cup (213 g) brown sugar

2 teaspoons vanilla extract

½ teaspoon salt

6 tablespoons (76 g) mini semisweet chocolate chips

6 tablespoons (76 g) finely chopped chocolate toffee bar (such as Heath Bar)

12 ounces (340 g) white chocolate candy melts, or in the colors of your choice

8 to 10 lollipop sticks (see note)

Rainbow sprinkles, for garnish

Toffee Crunch Cookie Dough Pops

Welcome to paradise, fellow devotees of raw cookie dough. You're in for an exceptional treat. We created a delicious—and safe to eat—chocolate chip cookie dough recipe that's the answer to all your prayers. Loaded with mini chocolate chips and crunchy bits of toffee, our celestial sticks are dipped in melted white chocolate that cools into cute candy shells. Topped with rainbow sprinkles, these heavenly pops are a taste of the divine.

Make the Dough: Preheat the oven to 350°F (177°C) and line a baking sheet with parchment paper. Spread the flour in an even layer on the parchment and bake for 5 to 10 minutes, or until the flour reaches 160°F (71°C) on a cooking thermometer. Allow the flour to cool for 5 minutes, then sift into a small bowl to remove any lumps. Set aside.

In a large mixing bowl, beat the butter and brown sugar on medium speed until light and fluffy. Add the vanilla and salt and beat until smooth. Add the flour and beat until no dry streaks remain. Add the mini chips and toffee and beat until evenly distributed in the dough. Scoop the dough into 1½-inch balls and place them on a plate in the fridge to firm up for 30 minutes.

Dip the Cookie Dough Pops: First, prepare a place to hold the cookie dough pops upright after dipping—you can use a block of Styrofoam, or a small cardboard box with holes cut in the top.

Place the chocolate candy melts in a small bowl and follow the package directions to melt them in the microwave.

Dip a lollipop stick about 1 inch into the melted chocolate to coat one end. Then insert the coated end into one of the chilled cookie dough balls. Cover the entire ball with melted chocolate, either by dipping it in the bowl, or by drizzling the chocolate over it. Allow the excess chocolate to drip back into the bowl, then place the stick on the prepared holder

to keep it upright. Sprinkle the top with rainbow sprinkles, then repeat with the remaining cookie dough balls. The white chocolate shell will dry in about 30 minutes at room temperature, or 10 minutes in the fridge. Enjoy!

Note: Lollipop sticks are available in arts and crafts stores and online.

2 sticks (226 g) unsalted butter,
at room temperature

½ cup (99 g) granulated sugar

½ teaspoon salt

Grated zest from 1 lemon

5 teaspoons lemon juice

1 teaspoon vanilla extract

2 cups (240 g) all-purpose flour

10 to 12 hard candies, in various
colors (such as Jolly Ranchers or
Life Savers)

Sour Lemon
Stained-Glass Stars

These cosmic cookies will light up the night. In this colorful recipe, crisp and buttery shortbread is baked with tangy lemon zest and cut into decorative stars. They're filled with crushed hard candies that melt in the oven, creating a constellation of brilliant stained-glass centers. Zesty and out-of-this-world delicious, these stellar sweets will disappear faster than a shooting star.

Make the Dough: In a large mixing bowl, beat the butter and sugar on medium speed until light and fluffy. Add the salt, lemon zest, lemon juice, and vanilla and beat until smooth. Add the flour and beat until no dry streaks remain. Gather the dough into a ball, then flatten slightly to make a disc shape, wrap tightly in plastic, and refrigerate for at least 2 hours. Dough can keep in the fridge for up to 1 week.

Bake the Cookies: Preheat the oven to 350°F (177°C) and line one or more baking sheets with parchment paper.

Unwrap the disc of dough and place it on a lightly floured work surface. Roll the dough to a large circle about ⅛ inch thick. The dough may crack slightly, so if this happens, gently press it back together as you roll. Using a 3-inch star cutter, cut out as many stars as possible from the dough. Then, using a 1-inch star cutter, cut out the centers of the cookies. Transfer the cookies to the prepared baking sheets, leaving about 1 inch of space between each one. Gather and reroll the dough scraps, then cut out the remaining cookies. Place the baking sheets in the freezer for 15 minutes; this helps the cookies keep their shape while baking.

Organize the hard candies by color. Crush the candies into small pieces one color at a time, placing them in separate bowls. They can be crushed using a mortar and pestle, or by placing the candies in a sealed bag and crushing them with a rolling pin. Note that the candies should be in small pieces, not ground into powder.

Continued...

Remove the sheets from the freezer. Fill the center of each cookie with crushed candies until it is about ¾ full, using one color per cookie. Once all the cookies are filled, bake for 10 to 12 minutes, until the edges of the cookies are lightly golden and the centers are bubbly. If baking two pans at once, swap the positions of the pans halfway through to ensure the cookies bake evenly.

Let the cookies cool on the baking sheet for 5 minutes, then transfer to a wire rack to cool completely. Enjoy!

Slice-and-Bake Raspberry Spirals

For the Cookies

2¼ cups (270 g) all-purpose flour

½ teaspoon baking powder

½ teaspoon salt

2 sticks (226 g) unsalted butter, at room temperature

¾ cup (149 g) granulated sugar

1 large egg, at room temperature

1 teaspoon vanilla extract

For the Raspberry Coconut Filling

½ cup (160 g) seedless raspberry jam (see note)

⅔ cup (64 g) sweetened shredded coconut

2 tablespoons powdered sugar

Round and round we go; where the raspberry stops, nobody knows. These cute sugar cookies are stylishly spiraled with a tangy raspberry coconut filling. They're lightly crisp on the outside, chewy in the middle, and couldn't be easier to prepare. Simply make the dough, spread it with jam, roll it up, then slice-and-bake. Hypnotize your friends with its spellbinding swirls and fantastic flavors—a splendid time is guaranteed for all!

Make the Dough: In a small bowl, whisk together the flour, baking powder, and salt. Set aside.

In a large mixing bowl, beat the butter and granulated sugar on medium speed until light and fluffy. Add the egg and vanilla and beat until smooth. Add the flour mixture and beat until no dry streaks remain. Gather the dough, then divide in half. Form each half into a brick shape, then flatten slightly to about 1 inch thick. Wrap tightly in plastic and refrigerate for at least 1 hour. Dough can keep in the fridge for up to 1 week.

Make the Filling and Roll the Dough: In a small bowl, stir together the jam, coconut, and powdered sugar until evenly blended. Set aside.

Unwrap one of the rectangles of dough and place it on a lightly floured work surface. Roll the dough to a 9 x 7-inch rectangle about ¼ inch thick. The dough may crack slightly, so if this happens, gently press it back together as you roll. Using a knife or pizza cutter, trim the edges to make a clean rectangular shape and discard the excess dough. Spread half the raspberry coconut filling over the dough, leaving ¼ inch of space around the edges. Carefully roll the dough tightly to a 9-inch log about 2 inches thick, then wrap in plastic. Repeat with the second half of dough and the remaining raspberry coconut filling. Place the two wrapped logs seam side down in the refrigerator for at least 1 hour. Dough can keep in the fridge for up to 1 week.

Continued . . .

Bake the Cookies: Preheat the oven to 350°F (177°C) and line one or more baking sheets with parchment paper.

Unwrap one of the logs of dough, and if the bottom has flattened a bit, gently squeeze the log until it becomes a perfect cylinder. Use a sharp knife to slice the log into ½-inch-thick circles. Place the circles on the prepared baking sheet, leaving 2 inches of space between each one and placing approximately 15 circles per sheet. Repeat with the remaining dough. Place the baking sheets in the freezer for 15 minutes; this helps the cookies keep their shape while baking.

Transfer the baking sheets directly to the oven and bake for 10 to 12 minutes, until the edges are lightly golden. If baking two pans at once, swap the positions of the pans halfway through to ensure the cookies bake evenly.

Let the cookies cool on the baking sheet for 5 minutes, then transfer to a wire rack to cool completely. Enjoy!

Note: Be sure to use seedless raspberry jam, as regular raspberry jam contains large amounts of seeds that impact the texture of the cookies. If seedless jam is unavailable, a fine-mesh strainer can be used to filter out the seeds instead.

Makes about 16 (2½-inch) cookies

Chocolate Rainbow Meltaways

Toto, we've a feeling we're not in Kansas anymore. These Technicolor treats are truly melt-in-your-mouth magnificent. Rich, dark, and ultrachocolaty, our chromatic cookies are topped with a psychedelic tie-dye glaze, and each one is a unique work of art. If you're a fan of fudgy confections, this dreamy dessert will take you on a tasty trip over the rainbow.

For the Cookies

½ cup (85 g) bittersweet chocolate chips (about 65% cacao)

3 tablespoons chopped unsweetened chocolate (100% cacao)

4 tablespoons (57 g) unsalted butter, cubed

½ cup (60 g) all-purpose flour

½ teaspoon baking powder

½ teaspoon salt

¾ cup (149 g) granulated sugar

2 large eggs, at room temperature

1 teaspoon vanilla extract

For the Rainbow Glaze

3 cups (339 g) powdered sugar

4½ tablespoons (67 ml) whole milk

¼ teaspoon plus ⅛ teaspoon salt

Red gel food coloring

Orange gel food coloring

Yellow gel food coloring

Green gel food coloring

Blue gel food coloring

Purple gel food coloring

Make the Dough: Fill a small saucepan with 1 to 2 inches of water and bring to a simmer over medium heat. Place a small heatproof bowl over the pan, so the bottom of the bowl rests above the surface of the simmering water. Place the bittersweet chips, unsweetened chocolate, and butter in the bowl and stir until melted and smooth with no lumps remaining. Carefully remove the hot bowl from the pan and set aside to cool for 5 to 10 minutes.

In a small bowl, whisk together the flour, baking powder, and ½ teaspoon salt. Set aside.

In a large mixing bowl, beat the granulated sugar and eggs on medium speed until light and foamy, 2 to 3 minutes. Add the vanilla and chocolate and beat until smooth. Add the flour mixture and beat until no dry streaks remain. Cover the bowl with plastic and refrigerate for at least 2 hours. Dough can keep in the fridge for up to 1 week.

Bake the Cookies: Preheat the oven to 350°F (177°C) and line one or more baking sheets with parchment paper.

Scoop about 2 tablespoons dough into a ball and place it on the prepared baking sheet. Repeat with the remaining dough, leaving 2 inches of space between each one.

Bake for 11 to 13 minutes, until the edges are set and the centers no longer appear wet. If baking two pans at once, swap the positions of the pans halfway through to ensure the cookies bake evenly. As soon as the pans come out of the oven, use a wide spatula to gently press down and slightly flatten the cookies.

134 That Takes the Cookie

Let the cookies cool on the baking sheet for 5 minutes, then transfer to a wire rack for 15 minutes to cool completely. Once cool, transfer the cookies to a sealed container in the fridge and refrigerate for at least 1 hour. Cookies can keep in the fridge for up to 1 week.

Glaze the Cookies: Sift the powdered sugar into a medium bowl, then add the milk and ¼ teaspoon plus ⅛ teaspoon salt and stir until smooth and blended with no lumps remaining.

Pour 2 tablespoons glaze into a small bowl, and add a few drops of red gel food coloring. Stir to blend, then continue to add color one drop at a time until the glaze is deep red. Set aside, then repeat the process with the remaining colors—orange, yellow, green, blue, and purple. When finished, you will have six small bowls of individually colored glazes. Set aside the remaining white glaze.

Pour 1 tablespoon white glaze into a small, shallow bowl, forming a pool about 3 inches wide. Pour about ¼ teaspoon red glaze onto the pool of white glaze, forming a patch of red color about 1 inch wide. Then, using a clean spoon, pour about ¼ teaspoon orange glaze next to the red, leaving a small white space (approximately ⅛ inch) between the two colors. Repeat with the remaining colors—yellow, green, blue, and purple—until the glaze is evenly divided among the six colors.

Dip the top of a cookie into the glaze, pressing it down to coat the cookie evenly. Then, holding the cookie by its edges, lift the cookie straight up without twisting or turning it, allowing the excess glaze to drip back into the bowl. Place the cookie on a wire rack to dry, then repeat with the remaining cookies, rinsing out the bowl and recoloring the glaze for each cookie, since the colors become messy and dark after dipping once. The glazed cookies will dry in 20 to 30 minutes. Enjoy!

1½ cups (255 g)
white chocolate chips

1½ cups (255 g)
butterscotch chips

1½ cups (255 g)
peanut butter chips

1 tablespoon
vegetable shortening

½ teaspoon
green food coloring

½ teaspoon
orange food coloring

½ teaspoon
purple food coloring

½ teaspoon
black food coloring

1 cup (138 g)
salted peanuts

6 cups (340 g) **crunchy
chow mein noodles**

**Candy eyes, for decoration
(see note)**

Note: Candy eyes are available in arts and crafts stores and online.

Haunted Halloween Haystacks

Looking for a spooky dessert for your next Halloween bash? These creepy, crunchy creatures will have your guests screaming with delight. Made with three kinds of melted chips—white chocolate, peanut butter, and butterscotch—this bewitching blend is then mixed with roasted peanuts, crispy chow mein noodles . . . and a teaspoon of terror befitting the holiday. It's a quick and easy, sweet and salty snack that's so scary good, it's frightening.

Line two baking sheets with parchment paper and set aside.

Fill a medium saucepan with 1 to 2 inches of water and bring to a simmer over medium heat. Place a large heat-proof bowl over the pan, so the bottom of the bowl rests above the surface of the simmering water. Place the chocolate chips, butterscotch chips, peanut butter chips, and shortening in the bowl and stir until melted and smooth with no lumps remaining. Divide the mixture evenly into four medium bowls. To each bowl, add one of the colors and stir to combine. To achieve a darker color, add a few drops of food coloring, as needed. To each bowl, add ¼ cup peanuts and 1½ cups chow mein noodles, breaking up the noodles with your hands as you add them. Stir until the noodles are evenly coated, then scoop about ¼ cup of the mixture onto the prepared baking sheet, forming a small mound about 3 inches wide. Repeat with the remaining mixture, leaving about 1 inch of space between each cookie. Garnish each cookie with 2 candy eyes, then place the sheets in the refrigerator and chill for 30 minutes until the cookies firm up. Remove from the fridge and serve at room temperature. Enjoy!

For the Cookies

2¼ cups (270 g) all-purpose flour

½ teaspoon baking powder

½ teaspoon salt

2 sticks (226 g) unsalted butter,
at room temperature

¾ cup (149 g) granulated sugar

1 large egg, at room temperature

1 teaspoon vanilla extract

For the Marshmallows (see note)

3 packets unflavored gelatin
powder (see note)

1 cup (237 ml) water

1½ cups (297 g) granulated sugar

1 cup (320 g) light corn syrup

¼ teaspoon salt

1 teaspoon vanilla extract

For the Strawberry
White Chocolate Shell

¾ cup (20 g) freeze-dried
strawberries

16 ounces (454 g) pink candy
melts

Strawberry Shortcake Marshmallow Cookies

Sure, everyone loves chocolate Mallomars, but wait till
you try our pretty-in-pink strawberry shortcake version.
Starting with a buttery, vanilla sugar cookie base, they're
crowned with pillow-soft, homemade marshmallow kisses,
then candy-coated in an irresistible strawberry white
chocolate shell. Need we say more?

Make the Dough: In a small bowl, whisk together the
flour, baking powder, and ½ teaspoon salt. Set aside.

In a large mixing bowl, beat the butter and ¾ cup sugar on
medium speed until light and fluffy. Add the egg and 1 teaspoon vanilla and beat until smooth. Add the flour mixture
and beat until no dry streaks remain. Gather the dough
into a ball, then flatten slightly to make a disc shape, wrap
tightly in plastic, and refrigerate for at least 2 hours. Dough
can keep in the fridge for up to 1 week.

Bake the Cookies: Preheat the oven to 350°F (177°C) and
line one or more baking sheets with parchment paper.

Unwrap the disc of dough and place it on a lightly floured
work surface. Roll the dough to a large circle about ¼ inch
thick. The dough may crack slightly, so if this happens,
gently press it back together as you roll. Using a 2-inch
circle cutter, cut out as many circles as possible from the
dough. Transfer the cookies to the prepared baking sheets,
leaving about 1 inch of space between each one. Gather and
reroll the dough scraps, then cut out the remaining cookies. Place the baking sheets in the freezer for 15 minutes;
this helps the cookies keep their shape while baking.

Transfer the baking sheets directly to the oven and bake for
10 to 12 minutes, until the edges of the cookies are lightly
golden. If baking two pans at once, swap the positions of the
pans halfway through to ensure the cookies bake evenly.

Let the cookies cool on the baking sheet for 5 minutes, then
transfer to a wire rack to cool completely.

Continued . . .

Make the Marshmallows: In the mixing bowl of an electric mixer, combine the gelatin with ½ cup water and stir to combine. Set aside.

In a small saucepan, combine the 1½ cups sugar, corn syrup, ¼ teaspoon salt, and ½ cup water. Place over medium-high heat and bring to a simmer, stirring occasionally. Continue to simmer until the mixture reaches 235° to 240°F (113° to 116°C) on a cooking thermometer. Remove the pan from the heat, then set the electric mixer to low speed using the whisk attachment. With the mixer running, pour the hot sugar syrup into the bowl of gelatin in a slow, steady stream—it should take about 1 minute to add all the syrup. Once all the syrup has been added, add the 1 teaspoon vanilla, then set the mixer to high speed and continue whipping for 7 to 10 minutes, until smooth and glossy.

Note: The gelatin packets should be 7 g or 2¼ teaspoons each.

If desired, use store-bought marshmallows to save time.

Transfer the marshmallow mixture to a piping bag fitted with a wide round tip and pipe marshmallow kisses on top of each cookie, covering the cookie in a rounded shape about 1 inch tall. Allow the marshmallows to dry on the cookies at room temperature until no longer sticky, 1 to 2 hours. Any extra marshmallow mixture left after topping all the cookies can be made into individual marshmallows by piping them directly onto a parchment-lined baking sheet, if desired.

Make the Strawberry White Chocolate Shell:

Arrange the marshmallow-topped cookies on wire racks and place baking sheets underneath.

Place the strawberries in a food processor and pulse until they become a finely ground powder. Set a fine-mesh strainer over a medium bowl and sift the powdered strawberries into the bowl, removing and discarding the seeds—you will end up with about 3 tablespoons strawberry powder. Set aside.

Place the candy melts in a small bowl and follow the package directions to melt them in the microwave. Once completely melted and smooth, add the strawberry powder and stir until evenly blended. Use a spoon or spatula to drizzle each cookie until evenly coated in a thin layer of melted chocolate. If the chocolate begins to cool and becomes too thick to drizzle, it can be reheated in the microwave as needed. The chocolate shell will harden in about 45 minutes at room temperature, or 5 to 10 minutes in the refrigerator. Serve at room temperature, and enjoy!

For the Cookies

1¾ cups (210 g) all-purpose flour

½ teaspoon baking powder

¼ teaspoon baking soda

¼ teaspoon salt

1¼ sticks (141 g) unsalted butter,
at room temperature

1 cup (198 g) granulated sugar

1 large egg, at room temperature

2 teaspoons vanilla extract

⅓ cup (76 g) sour cream,
at room temperature

For the Peppermint Glaze

2½ cups (283 g) powdered sugar

3 tablespoons whole milk

1 tablespoon light corn syrup

¼ teaspoon peppermint extract

⅛ teaspoon salt

Red gel food coloring

Green gel food coloring

Have Yourself a Merry Little Cookie

The holidays wouldn't be the same without cookies. It would be like celebrating Halloween without candy, or Thanksgiving dinner without pie. We created a classic Christmas cookie that's here to make everyone's spirits bright. Inspired by the legendary black and white cookie, our joyful treats are festively colored in two different styles with a cool peppermint glaze. Whether you choose the green and white combo or the red and white . . . have yourself a merry little cookie now.

Make the Dough: In a small bowl, whisk together the flour, baking powder, baking soda, and ¼ teaspoon salt. Set aside.

In a large mixing bowl, beat the butter and granulated sugar on medium speed until light and fluffy. Add the egg and vanilla and beat until smooth. Then add the sour cream and beat until combined. Add the flour mixture and beat until no dry streaks remain.

Bake the Cookies: Preheat the oven to 350°F (177°C) and line two baking sheets with parchment paper.

Scoop ¼ cup dough onto the prepared baking sheet, placing 5 cookies per sheet and spacing them 3 inches apart.

Bake for 13 to 15 minutes, until the edges of the cookies are lightly golden and the centers no longer appear wet. If baking two pans at once, swap the positions of the pans halfway through to ensure the cookies bake evenly.

Let the cookies cool on the baking sheet for 5 minutes, then transfer to a wire rack to cool completely.

Make the Glaze: Place a fine-mesh strainer over a medium bowl and sift the powdered sugar through the strainer into the bowl. Add the milk, corn syrup, peppermint extract, and ⅛ teaspoon salt and stir until smooth and evenly blended, with no lumps remaining.

Continued . . .

Pour ¼ cup glaze into one small bowl, and pour another ¼ cup glaze into a second small bowl. Add 1 to 2 drops red gel food coloring to the first bowl, and add 1 to 2 drops green gel food coloring to the second bowl. If deeper shades of color are desired, stir in one drop at a time until the desired color is reached. The remaining ½ cup glaze will be kept white. Cover the three bowls of glaze until ready to use so they don't dry out.

Glaze the Cookies: Keep the cookies on the wire rack and flip them over so the flat side faces up. Spread 2 teaspoons white glaze on one half of each cookie in a half-moon design. To get a perfectly straight line in the center, place a thin spatula in the middle of the cookie, making a barrier to prevent the glaze from spreading onto the other half. Allow the glaze to fully dry, about 20 minutes. Once the white glaze has dried, spread 2 teaspoons of either red or green glaze on the other half of each cookie. Allow the glaze to dry, about 20 minutes, then serve and enjoy!

Makes 14 to 16 (4-inch) cookies

8 ounces (226 g) cream cheese, at room temperature

2 sticks (226 g) unsalted butter, at room temperature

1 cup (113 g) powdered sugar

½ teaspoon salt

2 teaspoons vanilla extract

2 cups (240 g) all-purpose flour

6 tablespoons assorted jams (blueberry, strawberry, seedless raspberry, orange)

1 large egg, at room temperature

1 teaspoon water

Sparkling sugar, for garnish

Sparkling Party Pinwheels

Add some sparkle to your next gathering. These party pinwheels are cute . . . and colorful. Imagine a flaky, buttery, pastry-like, pinwheel-shaped cookie with a dollop of fruity jam in the middle. We fill ours with four fun fruit flavors—strawberry, blueberry, raspberry, and orange marmalade—then top the cookies with a shimmer of sparkling sugar. They make a delightful display and are party-perfect. Just don't forget to include us when you're sending out the invitations.

Make the Dough: In a large mixing bowl, beat the cream cheese, butter, powdered sugar, and salt on medium speed until light and fluffy. Then add the vanilla and beat until smooth. Add the flour and beat until no dry streaks remain. Gather the dough into a ball, then flatten slightly to make a disc shape, wrap tightly in plastic, and refrigerate for at least 2 hours. Dough can keep in the fridge for up to 1 week.

Bake the Cookies: Preheat the oven to 350°F (177°C) and line one or more baking sheets with parchment paper.

Unwrap the disc of dough and place it on a lightly floured work surface. Roll the dough to a large circle about ⅛ inch thick. The dough may crack slightly, so if this happens, gently press it back together as you roll. Cut the dough into 3-inch squares using a knife or pizza cutter, trimming any excess dough. Transfer the squares to the prepared baking sheets, leaving about 1 inch of space between each one. Gather and reroll the dough scraps, then cut out the remaining squares.

To create the pinwheel shape, use a sharp knife to make 1-inch cuts in the four corners of each square; the cuts should start at each corner and extend 1 inch toward the center of the square, forming an X shape and leaving the center area uncut. Spoon 1 teaspoon jam onto the center area of each square. Lift one of the corner pieces of dough

Continued . . .

and fold it toward the center, pressing the tip gently onto the jam. Work your way around the square, lifting and folding every other corner piece toward the center, creating a pinwheel shape. Repeat with the remaining squares.

In a small bowl or cup, whisk together the egg and 1 teaspoon water to create an egg wash. Use a small pastry brush to lightly coat the surface of the pinwheels with the egg wash—note that the egg wash can also be used to glue the center pieces of pastry together if the pinwheel begins to unfold its shape. Then, sprinkle sparkling sugar over the cookies until they are evenly coated. Place the baking sheets in the freezer for 15 minutes; this helps the cookies keep their shape while baking.

Transfer the baking sheets directly to the oven and bake for 13 to 15 minutes, until the edges of the cookies are golden brown. If baking two pans at once, swap the positions of the pans halfway through to ensure the cookies bake evenly.

Let the cookies cool on the baking sheet for 10 minutes, then transfer to a wire rack to cool completely. Enjoy!

Note: Be sure to use seedless raspberry jam, as regular raspberry jam contains large amounts of seeds that impact the texture of the cookies. If seedless jam is unavailable, a fine-mesh strainer can be used to filter out the seeds instead.

chapter 5

cookies
'round the
world

Pack your suitcase. You're invited to join us for a once-in-a-lifetime cookie tour 'round the world! We'll visit Italy and learn the secret to making classic, chewy Lemon Olive Oil Pignoli (page 152). We'll fly over the Andes to Argentina and learn the trick to baking perfectly soft Alfajores with Dulce de Leche (page 165), then we'll sail to the Greek Isles to taste the celebrated Melomakarona Spiced Honey Cookies (page 159) prepared during Christmastime. This dessert excursion will feature sixteen international destinations, for the sweetest sightseeing (and sight-eating) you'll ever experience, and That Takes the Cookie. All aboard!

Makes

10 to 12
(3-inch)
cookies

For the Cookies

½ cup (107 g) brown sugar

½ cup (118 ml) water

2½ sticks (283 g) unsalted butter, cubed

3¾ cups (450 g) all-purpose flour

1½ teaspoons baking powder

¼ teaspoon salt

For the Filling and Assembly

½ cup (107 g) brown sugar

1 tablespoon all-purpose flour

1 large egg

1 teaspoon water

Sparkling sugar, for garnish

Coyotas de Sonora

¡Felicidades! You've just struck gold. These mini empanada-like cookies from Sonora, Mexico, are certainly something to celebrate. Golden and flaky on the outside and filled with dark brown sugar in the middle, this traditional northwestern Mexican pastry is also sprinkled with sparkling sugar, bringing all the pizazz to the party. Feeling generous? Share the wealth and bake a batch today. *¡Disfruten y buen provecho!*

Make the Dough: In a small saucepan, combine the ½ cup brown sugar and ½ cup water. Set over medium heat and stir until the sugar dissolves. Then add the butter and stir until melted and smooth. Remove from the heat and let cool for 5 minutes.

In a large mixing bowl, whisk together the 3¾ cups flour, baking powder, and salt. Add the brown sugar mixture and stir to combine. If using an electric mixer, use the dough hook attachment to knead until the dough is smooth, stretchy, and pulls away cleanly from the sides of the bowl, about 5 minutes. If kneading by hand, transfer the dough to a lightly floured work surface and knead until smooth and stretchy, about 10 minutes—note that the dough is quite wet and loose at first, but just keep kneading and it will reach a stretchy consistency after several minutes; you shouldn't need to add additional flour. Gather the dough into a ball, then flatten slightly to make a disc shape. Wrap tightly in plastic and refrigerate for at least 2 hours. Dough can keep in the fridge for up to 1 week.

Make the Filling and Bake the Cookies: Preheat the oven to 350°F (177°C) and line a baking sheet with parchment paper.

In a small bowl, stir together the ½ cup brown sugar and 1 tablespoon flour until evenly mixed with no lumps remaining. Set aside.

Unwrap the disc of dough and place it on a lightly floured work surface. Roll the dough to a large circle about ⅛ inch

150 That Takes the Cookie

thick. Using a 3-inch circle cutter, cut out as many circles as possible from the dough. Place one circle on the prepared baking sheet and scoop 2 teaspoons brown sugar filling in the center in a tight mound, leaving about ½ inch of space clear around the edges. Place a second circle on top, gently pressing the edges together to seal the filling inside. Use a fork to decoratively crimp the edges and also poke a few small holes in the top of the cookie. Repeat with the remaining circles of dough, leaving about 2 inches of space between each cookie on the baking sheet.

In a small bowl or measuring cup, whisk together the egg and 1 teaspoon water. Use a pastry brush to lightly coat the top and sides of the cookies in egg wash, then sprinkle each one with generous pinches of sparkling sugar.

Transfer the sheets to the oven and bake for 25 to 30 minutes, until the tops of the cookies are lightly golden brown. If baking two pans at once, swap the positions of the pans halfway through to ensure the cookies bake evenly.

Let the cookies cool on the baking sheet for 5 minutes, then transfer to a wire rack to cool completely. Enjoy!

1½ cups (397 g) almond paste
(see note)

1 cup (198 g) granulated sugar

1 cup (113 g) powdered sugar,
plus more for dusting

2 tablespoons grated lemon zest
(from about 4 lemons)

½ teaspoon salt

2 tablespoons extra-virgin olive oil

2 large egg whites, at room
temperature

¾ cup (105 g) pine nuts

Note: Almond paste is sold
in the baking aisle of many
grocery stores and online.
Do not use marzipan, which
has a higher sugar content
than almond paste.

Lemon Olive Oil Pignoli

Buckle your seat belts and prepare for takeoff! The next stop on our cookie caravan is Italy. Pignoli are popular southern Italian cookies known for their exceptional chewiness and delicate almond flavor. With our sunny Southern California version, we add a hint of lemon zest and a splash of extra-virgin olive oil for a bright and citrusy take on this Sicilian classic. Topped with golden pine nuts and a light dusting of powdered sugar, these soft and airy cookies are simple to make. So what are you waiting for? Stop reading and start baking! *Buon appetito!*

Make the Dough: Using your hands, break up the almond paste into a food processor, then add the granulated sugar, powdered sugar, lemon zest, and salt. Pulse until combined and no lumps remain. Add the olive oil and egg whites and process until smooth and evenly blended. Transfer the dough to a medium bowl.

Bake the Cookies: Preheat the oven to 325°F (163°C) and line one or more baking sheets with parchment paper.

Scoop about 2 tablespoons dough into a ball and place it on the prepared baking sheet. Repeat with the remaining dough, leaving 2 inches of space between each one and placing approximately 12 dough balls per sheet. Gently press the pine nuts onto the surface of each mound of dough, using 1 to 1½ teaspoons pine nuts per cookie.

Bake for 15 to 20 minutes, until the edges are lightly golden and the centers no longer appear wet. If baking two pans at once, swap the positions of the pans halfway through to ensure the cookies bake evenly.

Let the cookies cool on the baking sheet for 5 minutes, then transfer to a wire rack to cool completely. Lightly dust the cookies with powdered sugar, and enjoy!

2 sticks (226 g) unsalted butter,
at room temperature

¾ cup (149 g) granulated sugar

¾ teaspoon salt

1 tablespoon grated lime zest
(from about 2 limes)

1 large egg, at room temperature

1 teaspoon vanilla extract

2¾ cups (330 g) all-purpose flour

¾ cup (255 g) guava paste

Torticas de Morón
with Guava Filling

The pairing of guava and lime makes everything sublime.
These simple shortbread cookies are a Caribbean delight.
Buttery, crumbly, and infused with tangy lime zest, each
cookie is filled with a dollop of sweet guava paste in the
middle. Originating in Morón, Cuba, these traditional
treats go perfectly with your favorite Cuban music. Pour
yourself a mojito and let the fiesta begin! ¡Salud!

Make the Dough: In a large mixing bowl, beat the butter,
sugar, and salt on medium speed until light and fluffy. Add
the lime zest, egg, and vanilla and beat until smooth. Add
the flour and beat until no dry streaks remain. Cover the
bowl with plastic and refrigerate for at least 2 hours. Dough
can keep in the fridge for up to 1 week.

Bake the Cookies: Preheat the oven to 350°F (177°C) and
line one or more baking sheets with parchment paper.

Scoop 1 tablespoon dough into a ball and place it on the
prepared baking sheet. Repeat with the remaining dough,
leaving 2 inches of space between each one and placing
approximately 12 dough balls per sheet. Use your thumb to
create a well in the center of each cookie large enough to
hold 1 teaspoon filling. Spoon 1 teaspoon guava paste into
the center of each cookie. Place the baking sheets in the
freezer for 15 minutes; this helps the cookies keep their
shape while baking.

Transfer the baking sheets directly to the oven and bake for
12 to 14 minutes, until the edges are golden. If baking two
pans at once, swap the positions of the pans halfway through
to ensure the cookies bake evenly.

Let the cookies cool on the baking sheet for 5 minutes, then
transfer to a wire rack to cool completely. Enjoy!

Makes

48 to 50
(1-inch)
squares

Chocolate Espresso Millionaire's Shortbread

For the Shortbread Layer

2 sticks (226 g) unsalted butter, at room temperature

½ cup (99 g) granulated sugar

½ teaspoon salt

1¾ cups (210 g) all-purpose flour

For the Caramel Layer

1 (14-ounce/396 g) can sweetened condensed milk

¾ cup (160 g) brown sugar

4 tablespoons (57 g) unsalted butter, cubed

3 tablespoons light corn syrup

¾ teaspoon salt

For the Chocolate Espresso Layer

8 ounces (226 g) semisweet chocolate chips

1 teaspoon instant coffee crystals

1 teaspoon finely chopped coffee beans

Edible gold leaf, for garnish (optional, see note)

Fancify your festivities with these treasured treats from Scotland. Three luxurious layers are stacked high, creating a baked biscuit that tastes like a million bucks. It begins with a classic, buttery shortbread that is topped with golden chewy caramel, then a layer of rich coffee-infused chocolate. Sprinkled with chopped roasted coffee beans and garnished with gold leaf, these swanky squares are pure extravagance. *Sláinte!*

Make the Shortbread Layer: Preheat the oven to 350°F (177°C) and line an 8-inch square baking dish with two overlapping pieces of parchment paper placed perpendicular to each other. The pieces of parchment should be long enough to cover the bottom and sides of the pan and hang over the edges by an inch or two. This creates a sling to easily lift the bars out later.

In a large mixing bowl, beat the 2 sticks butter, granulated sugar, and ½ teaspoon salt on medium speed until light and fluffy. Add the flour and beat until no dry streaks remain. Gather the dough, then transfer to the prepared baking pan, pressing and spreading it all the way to the edges in an even layer.

Bake for 25 to 30 minutes, until the edges are golden brown and the top of the shortbread has a faint golden color. Remove the pan from the oven, place it on a wire rack, and immediately use a wide, flat spatula to gently press down and slightly compress the shortbread in the pan. This helps solidify the cookie and keeps it from becoming too crumbly. Allow the pan of shortbread to cool for about 20 minutes, until warm but no longer hot.

Make the Caramel Layer: In a small saucepan, combine the condensed milk, brown sugar, 4 tablespoons butter,

Continued . . .

Note: Gold leaf is available in arts and crafts stores and online.

corn syrup, and ¾ teaspoon salt. Set over medium-high heat and bring to a simmer, stirring with a silicone spatula and scraping the sides often to prevent scorching. Continue to simmer, stirring constantly, until the temperature reaches 225°F (107°C) on a cooking thermometer. Remove the pan from the heat and immediately pour the hot caramel over the shortbread. Spread the caramel all the way to the edges in an even layer. Allow the caramel to cool at room temperature until solidified, at least 60 minutes.

Make the Chocolate Espresso Layer: Fill a small saucepan with 1 to 2 inches of water and bring to a simmer over medium heat. Place a small heatproof bowl over the pan, so the bottom of the bowl rests above the surface of the simmering water. Place the chocolate chips and coffee crystals in the bowl and stir until melted and smooth with no lumps remaining. Remove the bowl from the pan and pour the chocolate onto the caramel, spreading the chocolate all the way to the edges in an even layer. Sprinkle the chocolate with the coffee beans, then transfer the pan to the refrigerator. Chill until the chocolate is set and no longer appears shiny and wet, 30 to 40 minutes.

Use the parchment sling to lift the shortbread out of the pan, then place it on a cutting board and remove the paper. Allow the shortbread to rest at room temperature for about 15 minutes before cutting. For best results, use a long, serrated knife to cut into 1-inch bars, using gentle sawing motions to help minimize crumbles in the shortbread. If desired, top each square with a small garnish of gold leaf. Store and serve the bars at room temperature, and enjoy!

For the Spiced Honey Syrup

1 cup (198 g) granulated sugar

1 cup (237 ml) water

1 whole cinnamon stick

½ teaspoon whole cloves

½ orange, unpeeled

½ cup (168 g) honey

For the Cookies

2½ to 3 cups (300 to 360 g)
all-purpose flour

¾ teaspoon ground cinnamon

½ teaspoon baking powder

¼ teaspoon plus ⅛ teaspoon salt

¼ teaspoon baking soda

¼ teaspoon ground cloves

¾ cup (177 ml) extra-virgin
olive oil

¼ cup (50 g) granulated sugar

6 tablespoons (89 ml) freshly
squeezed orange juice

Grated zest from ½ an orange

1½ tablespoons bourbon or
whiskey

¼ cup (84 g) honey, for garnish

1 cup (113 g) finely chopped
walnuts, for garnish

Melomakarona Spiced Honey Cookies

All hands on deck; we're setting our sails for the Mediterranean. These Greek cookies are an odyssey of flavor. Made with cinnamon, cloves, orange zest, and a splash of bourbon, they're baked until crisp and golden, then dipped in an aromatic spiced honey syrup. Garnished with finely chopped walnuts and a drizzle of honey, this dessert—traditionally made around Christmas—is boatloads of fun to make . . . and even more fun to eat. *Yiamas!*

Make the Spiced Honey Syrup: In a small saucepan, combine the 1 cup sugar, water, cinnamon stick, and whole cloves. Stir to dissolve the sugar, then place the orange cut side down in the pan. Set over medium heat and bring to a simmer, stirring occasionally. Reduce the heat and simmer for 10 minutes. Remove the pan from the heat, remove the orange half, then stir in the ½ cup honey until blended. Pour the hot syrup through a fine-mesh strainer into a heatproof bowl to remove the spices, then cover the bowl or transfer the syrup to a glass jar and refrigerate for at least 1 to 2 hours to chill. Syrup can keep in the fridge for up to 1 week.

Make the Dough: In a small bowl, whisk together 1 cup (120 g) of the flour with the ground cinnamon, baking powder, salt, baking soda, and ground cloves. Set aside.

In a large mixing bowl, combine the olive oil, ¼ cup sugar, orange juice, orange zest, and bourbon and beat until smooth. Add the spiced flour mixture and beat until blended. Begin adding more flour a few tablespoons at a time, beating between each addition, just until the mixture forms into a smooth dough that pulls away cleanly from the sides of the bowl—you will probably not use all the flour. Cover the bowl with plastic and refrigerate for at least 2 hours. Dough can keep in the fridge for up to 1 week.

Bake the Cookies: Preheat the oven to 350°F (177°C) and line one or more baking sheets with parchment paper.

Continued . . .

Scoop about 1 tablespoon dough into a ball, form it into an oval shape, and place it on the prepared baking sheet. Repeat with the remaining dough, leaving 1 inch of space between each one.

Bake for 20 to 25 minutes, until the bottom edges of the cookies are golden brown. If baking two pans at once, swap the positions of the pans halfway through to ensure the cookies bake evenly. As soon as the cookies come out of the oven, use a toothpick to poke three holes in the top of each cookie, then let cool on the baking sheet for 5 minutes.

While the cookies are cooling, pour the honey syrup into a bowl and place a wire rack over a baking sheet.

Using a fork or slotted spoon, dip a cookie in the syrup and keep it submerged for 15 seconds. Then place the cookie on the prepared rack to dry and repeat with the remaining cookies. Once all the cookies have been dipped, drizzle each one with ¼ to ½ teaspoon of honey and top with a sprinkle of walnuts. Enjoy!

Note: Don't discard the remaining Spiced Honey Syrup—it can be used as a flavorful ingredient to make delicious cocktails!

Coconut Polvorones with Ube Frosting

Our cookie quest continues to the Philippines. Have you ever tried an ube-flavored dessert before? Ube is a pretty purple yam (pronounced "oo-bay") with a sweet, nutty flavor, and is a staple of Filipino cuisine. Here, it's featured in a silky-smooth frosting, generously spread onto a traditional Polvoron cookie. These easy no-bake treats are quick to prepare: you just toast some flour in a skillet, then mix it with five other ingredients—butter, sugar, salt, powdered milk, and shredded coconut—and that's it. The dough is pressed into circles and chilled in the freezer, then they're ready to serve. Topped with a purple swirl of ube frosting and a sprinkle of shredded coconut, these vibrant cookies are decorative and delectable. *Tara! Kain!*

For the Cookies

2 cups (240 g) all-purpose flour

1 cup (198 g) granulated sugar

⅛ teaspoon salt

1 cup (80 g) powdered milk (see note)

⅓ cup (36 g) sweetened shredded coconut, finely chopped

2 sticks (226 g) unsalted butter, melted

For the Ube Frosting

1½ sticks (170 g) unsalted butter, at room temperature

1½ cups (170 g) powdered sugar

⅛ teaspoon salt (heaping)

1 to 1½ teaspoons ube extract (see note)

⅓ cup (36 g) sweetened shredded coconut, finely chopped, for garnish

Make the Cookies: Line one or more baking sheets with parchment paper and set aside.

Place the flour in a large skillet and set over medium-low heat. Cook the flour until toasted and fragrant, 12 to 15 minutes, stirring often to prevent scorching. Immediately transfer the flour to a heatproof bowl or plate to cool for 5 minutes.

Sift the toasted flour into a large mixing bowl to remove any lumps. Add the granulated sugar, ⅛ teaspoon salt, powdered milk, and ⅓ cup coconut and stir to combine. Add the 2 sticks butter and stir until evenly blended.

Place a 2-inch circle cutter on the prepared baking sheet. Scoop 2 tablespoons dough into the center of the circle cutter, then firmly press the dough until it fills the cutter in a compressed, even layer about ½ inch thick. Gently lift the circle cutter, leaving the cookie on the baking sheet. Repeat with the remaining dough, leaving less than 1 inch of space between each cookie since they do not bake. (Alternatively, you could also form the cookies in a paper-lined cupcake pan, pressing the dough into the cupcake cups, then removing the paper before frosting.) Place the cookies in the freezer for 30 minutes to firm up.

Continued . . .

Note: Ube extract is available in Filipino grocery stores or can be purchased online.

Powdered milk is available in the baking aisle of most grocery stores and online.

Make the Frosting and Assemble the Cookies:

Place the 1½ sticks butter in a large mixing bowl. Sift the powdered sugar into the bowl to remove any lumps, then beat on medium speed until light and fluffy. Add the ⅛ teaspoon salt and 1 teaspoon ube extract and beat until smooth, blended, and vibrantly purple. If needed, add more ube extract a few drops at a time to achieve the desired color.

Top each cookie with about 2 teaspoons frosting, spreading it into an even layer, then garnish with a sprinkle of coconut. Enjoy!

For the Dulce de Leche

1 (14-ounce/396 g) can sweetened condensed milk (see note)

For the Cookies

1 cup (120 g) all-purpose flour

1 cup (113 g) cornstarch

1 teaspoon baking powder

¼ teaspoon baking soda

¼ teaspoon salt

1½ sticks (170 g) unsalted butter, at room temperature

⅔ cup (132 g) granulated sugar

2 large egg yolks, at room temperature

1 tablespoon heavy cream

1 teaspoon grated lemon zest

1 teaspoon vanilla extract

Powdered sugar, for dusting

Alfajores with Dulce de Leche

Pack your bags and bring an appetite—our tour of treats is taking us to Argentina. In this popular South American recipe, two extra-soft cookies are baked with lemon zest and vanilla, and then pressed together with a smooth layer of homemade dulce de leche. These irresistible sandwiches are dusted with powdered sugar and practically melt in your mouth. Make sure there's extra room in your luggage, since you'll be stuffing cookies in by the dozen. *¡Buen provecho!*

Make the Dulce de Leche: Remove the label from the can of condensed milk, then place the entire unopened can on its side in a large, deep pot. Note: placing the can on its side prevents it from banging around in the pan once the water is at a rolling boil. Fill the pot with water so the surface of the water is several inches above the top of the can. Cover the pan, set over high heat, and bring to a boil. Then lower the heat and simmer gently for 3 hours, periodically lifting the lid to make sure the water line stays at least 2 inches above the top of the can, and adding more boiling water, if needed, to keep the can fully submerged for important safety reasons (see note).

Use tongs to remove the hot can from the water and place it on a wire rack to fully cool to room temperature. For safety reasons, do not attempt to open the can while it is hot.

Make the Dough: In a small bowl, whisk together the flour, cornstarch, baking powder, baking soda, and salt. Set aside.

In a large mixing bowl, beat the butter and granulated sugar on medium speed until light and fluffy. Add the egg yolks, heavy cream, lemon zest, and vanilla and beat until smooth. Add the flour mixture and beat until no dry streaks remain. Gather the dough into a ball, then flatten slightly to make a disc shape. Wrap tightly in plastic and refrigerate for at least 2 hours. Dough can keep in the fridge for up to 1 week.

Continued...

Bake the Cookies: Preheat the oven to 350°F (177°C) and line one or more baking sheets with parchment paper.

Unwrap the disc of dough and place it on a lightly floured work surface. Roll the dough to a large circle about ¼ inch thick. The dough may crack slightly, so if this happens, gently press it back together as you roll. Using a 1½-inch circle cutter, cut out as many circles as possible from the dough. Transfer the cookies to the prepared baking sheets, leaving about 2 inches of space between each one. Gather and reroll the dough scraps, then cut out the remaining cookies. Place the baking sheets in the freezer for 15 minutes; this helps the cookies keep their shape while baking.

Transfer the baking sheets directly to the oven and bake for 8 to 11 minutes, until the edges of the cookies are lightly golden and the centers no longer appear wet. If baking two pans at once, swap the positions of the pans halfway through to ensure the cookies bake evenly.

Let the cookies cool on the baking sheet for 5 minutes, then transfer to a wire rack to cool completely.

Assemble the Cookies: Place one cookie flat side up, and spread about 2 teaspoons dulce de leche over it in an even layer. Place a second cookie flat side down on top to make a sandwich. Dust the cookies with powdered sugar, and enjoy!

Note: When boiling the can of condensed milk, it is absolutely vital that the water level stays several inches above the top of the can at all times. If the water in the pan evaporates, the pressure inside the can may cause it to explode.

Instead of making home-made dulce de leche, you could simply buy a can of prepared dulce de leche, commonly found in the Latin section of many grocery stores.

For the Cookies

2¼ cups (270 g) all-purpose flour

1 teaspoon ground cinnamon

½ teaspoon baking soda

½ teaspoon ground anise

½ teaspoon ground black pepper

¼ teaspoon salt

¼ teaspoon ground cloves

¼ teaspoon ground nutmeg

¼ teaspoon ground ginger

⅛ teaspoon ground cardamom

⅛ teaspoon ground allspice

4 tablespoons (57 g) unsalted butter, at room temperature

½ cup (107 g) brown sugar

¼ cup (85 g) molasses

3 tablespoons honey

1 large egg, at room temperature

For the Glaze

2 cups (226 g) powdered sugar

7 teaspoons water

½ teaspoon vanilla extract

Vanilla-Glazed Pfeffernüsse

Willkommen to Germany! Pfeffernüsse ("peppernuts") are soft spice cookies with flavors similar to gingerbread. The difference is that these are sweetened with honey and spiked with anise, cardamom, and even a hint of freshly ground black pepper, from which they get their name. Throughout the country, there are countless pfeffernüsse variations, but in northern Germany, they're often coated in a smooth vanilla glaze. With bold flavors and a cake-like texture, these Teutonic treats are truly tempting. *Prost!*

Make the Dough: In a medium bowl, whisk together the flour, cinnamon, baking soda, anise, black pepper, salt, cloves, nutmeg, ginger, cardamom, and allspice. Set aside.

In a medium saucepan, combine the butter, brown sugar, molasses, honey, and egg and stir to combine. Set over medium-low heat and continue to stir until the butter melts and the mixture is smooth and evenly blended. Remove the pan from the heat, then add the flour mixture and stir until no dry streaks remain. Transfer the dough to a heatproof bowl, then cover and refrigerate for at least 2 hours. Dough can keep in the fridge for up to 1 week.

Bake the Cookies: Preheat the oven to 350°F (177°C) and line one or more baking sheets with parchment paper.

Scoop about 1 tablespoon dough into a ball and place it on the prepared baking sheet. Repeat with the remaining dough, leaving 1 inch of space between each one.

Bake for 12 to 15 minutes, until the bottom edges of the cookies are golden brown and the tops no longer appear wet. If baking two pans at once, swap the positions of the pans halfway through to ensure the cookies bake evenly.

Let the cookies cool on the baking sheet for 5 minutes, then transfer to a wire rack to cool completely.

Continued . . .

Glaze the Cookies: In a medium bowl, whisk together the powdered sugar, water, and vanilla. Stir until smooth and creamy.

Place one of the cookies on a fork or slotted spoon and hold it above the bowl of glaze. Spoon a generous tablespoon of glaze over the cookie, allowing the excess to drip back into the bowl. Once the glaze stops dripping, transfer the cookie to a wire rack to dry. Repeat with the remaining cookies. The glaze will dry in 20 to 30 minutes. Enjoy!

1 medium sweet potato
(about 12 ounces/340 g)

1⅓ cups (160 g) all-purpose flour

2 teaspoons baking powder

½ cup (107 g) brown sugar

4 tablespoons (57 g) unsalted
butter, melted

2 tablespoons milk of your choice

1 tablespoon granulated sugar

1½ teaspoons ground cinnamon

½ teaspoon salt

½ cup (75 g) raisins

Mbatata (Sweet Potato Spice Cookies)

Do you believe in love at first bite? Well, you certainly will after trying these puffy, pillow-soft, heart-shaped treats. Malawi is known as the warm heart of Africa, and the traditional shape of these cookies is a tribute to their spirit of hospitality. *Mbatata* means "sweet potato" in the Chichewa language, and the golden color of these cookies comes from sweet potatoes that are blended into the dough, which is also filled with plump raisins and baked with brown sugar and cinnamon. Subtly sweet and made with kindness, you can taste the love in every bite. *Karibu!*

Make the Dough: Peel the sweet potato and cut into ½-inch cubes. Place the cubes in a medium saucepan and add enough water to cover the potatoes by a few inches. Bring to a boil, then lower the heat to a simmer and cook until the potatoes are tender when pierced with a fork, about 15 minutes. Drain the potatoes, then transfer to a bowl and mash until smooth. Measure 1 cup (240 g) of sweet potatoes and set aside. Any remaining mashed sweet potato can be saved for another use.

In a small bowl, whisk together the flour and baking powder. Set aside.

In a large mixing bowl, beat the 1 cup sweet potatoes, brown sugar, butter, milk, granulated sugar, cinnamon, and salt on medium speed until smooth and blended. Add the flour mixture and beat until no dry streaks remain. Add the raisins and beat until evenly distributed in the dough.

Gather the dough into a ball, wrap tightly in plastic, press into a flat disc shape, and refrigerate for at least 2 hours. Dough can keep in the fridge for up to 1 week.

Bake the Cookies: Preheat the oven to 350°F (177°C) and line one or more baking sheets with parchment paper.

Unwrap the disc of dough and place it on a lightly floured

Continued . . .

work surface. Roll the dough to a large circle between ¼ inch and ½ inch thick. Using a 3-inch heart cutter, cut out as many hearts as possible from the dough. Transfer the cookies to the prepared baking sheets, leaving about 2 inches of space between each one. Gather and reroll the dough scraps, then cut out the remaining cookies. Place the baking sheets in the freezer for 15 minutes; this helps the cookies keep their shape while baking.

Transfer the baking sheets directly to the oven and bake for 15 to 17 minutes, until the bottoms of the cookies are golden brown and the centers are puffy. If baking two pans at once, swap the positions of the pans halfway through to ensure the cookies bake evenly.

Let the cookies cool on the baking sheet for 5 minutes, then transfer to a wire rack to cool completely. Enjoy!

Makes

16 to 20
(3-inch)
cookies

Apricot-Pear Rugelach

Not a morning person? You will be now. These popular Polish pastries are here to help you start your day off right. Rugelach—or "little twists" in Yiddish—are flaky, buttery, crescent-shaped cookies that can be filled in a variety of ways. We spread ours with homemade pear butter infused with cinnamon, vanilla, nutmeg, and cloves, then sprinkle it with a brown-sugar-cinnamon crumble made with finely chopped walnuts and dried apricots. Pour yourself a cup of hot coffee, enjoy a rugelach—or three— and let these traditional Jewish treats melt your morning blues away. *L'chaim!*

**For the Pear Butter
(makes about 1½ cups)**

**4 firm, ripe pears
(about 260 g each)**

¾ cup (160 g) brown sugar

¼ cup (50 g) granulated sugar

1 tablespoon lemon juice

½ teaspoon vanilla extract

¼ teaspoon ground cinnamon

¼ teaspoon ground nutmeg

¼ teaspoon ground cloves

Pinch of salt

For the Dough

1 cup (120 g) all-purpose flour

¼ teaspoon salt

**4 ounces (113 g) cream cheese,
at room temperature**

**1 stick (113 g) unsalted butter,
at room temperature**

Make the Pear Butter: Cut the pears in quarters and remove the cores and stems. Place the pears in a large saucepan and add about ½ cup water to the pan. Cover and bring to a simmer over medium heat and cook without stirring for about 20 minutes, until the pears have softened. Using tongs, remove the pears from the pan, transfer them to a blender, and blend until smooth. Discard any water remaining in the pan.

Pour the pureed pears back into the empty saucepan, then add the ¾ cup brown sugar, granulated sugar, lemon juice, vanilla, ¼ teaspoon cinnamon, nutmeg, cloves, and a pinch of salt. Stir to combine, then set over medium heat and bring to a simmer, stirring often. Lower the heat to a bare simmer, and continue stirring occasionally for about 1 hour, until the mixture darkens and thickens to a smooth, spreadable paste. Once it has thickened to your liking, transfer it to a heatproof jar or container (you will have about 1½ cups pear butter), and keep refrigerated until ready to use. Pear butter will keep in the fridge for up to 2 weeks.

Make the Dough: In a small bowl, whisk together the flour and ¼ teaspoon salt. Set aside.

In a large mixing bowl, beat the cream cheese and butter on medium speed until light and fluffy. Add the flour mixture and beat until no dry streaks remain. Gather the dough, then

Continued...

174 That Takes the Cookie

For the Filling and Assembly

2 tablespoons brown sugar

¾ teaspoon ground cinnamon

¼ cup (28 g) finely chopped walnuts

¼ cup (50 g) finely chopped dried apricots

1 large egg

1 teaspoon water

Sparkling sugar, for garnish

Note: The extra pear butter can be spread on toast, enjoyed with pancakes or waffles, or simply eaten by the spoonful.

Don't have the time to prepare homemade pear butter? No problem! Store-bought pear butter or even apple butter will work just as well.

divide in half. Roll each half into a ball, then flatten slightly to make a disc shape. Wrap each disc tightly in plastic and refrigerate for at least 2 hours. Dough can keep in the fridge for up to 1 week.

Make the Filling and Bake the Cookies: Preheat the oven to 350°F (177°C) and line one or more baking sheets with parchment paper.

In a small bowl, stir together the 2 tablespoons brown sugar, ¾ teaspoon cinnamon, walnuts, and apricots. Set aside.

Unwrap one of the discs of dough and place it on a lightly floured work surface. Roll the dough to a 9-inch circle about ⅛ inch thick. Scoop ⅓ cup pear butter onto the dough, spreading it evenly and leaving ½ inch of space empty around the edge of the circle. Use a pastry cutter or large knife to cut the circle into 8 to 10 slices. Sprinkle half of the walnut-apricot mixture over the pear butter in an even layer. Slide a small spatula or butter knife under one of the slices and gently lift it away from the rest of the circle. Starting at the wide end, roll the slice until it creates a croissant-like pastry roll. Repeat with the remaining slices, then transfer the cookies to the prepared baking sheet, leaving about 2 inches of space between each one. Repeat the process with the second disc of dough.

In a small bowl, whisk together the egg and 1 teaspoon water until blended. Use a pastry brush to lightly coat the rugelach with egg wash until evenly moistened, then sprinkle them with sparkling sugar. Place the baking sheets in the freezer for 15 minutes; this helps the cookies keep their shape while baking.

Transfer the baking sheets directly to the oven and bake for 15 to 20 minutes, until golden brown. If baking two pans at once, swap the positions of the pans halfway through to ensure the cookies bake evenly.

Let the cookies cool on the baking sheet for 5 minutes, then transfer to a wire rack to cool completely. Enjoy!

Makes

38 to 40
(3-inch)
cookies

Macadamia-Coconut Shortbread with Passionfruit Glaze

For the Cookies

2¼ cups (270 g) all-purpose flour

½ teaspoon salt

½ teaspoon baking powder

2 sticks (226 g) unsalted butter, at room temperature

¾ cup (149 g) granulated sugar

1 large egg, at room temperature

1 teaspoon vanilla extract

¾ cup (90 g) macadamia nuts, finely chopped

2 tablespoons sweetened shredded coconut, finely chopped, plus more for garnish

For the Glaze

2 cups (226 g) powdered sugar

3 to 4 tablespoons seedless passionfruit puree (see note)

Our 'round-the-world itinerary wouldn't be complete without a stop in the magical islands of Hawaii. If you've never visited those rejuvenating isles, let these coconut cookies be your ticket to paradise. Starting with a buttery, crumbly shortbread speckled with macadamia nuts and finely chopped coconut, these Polynesian cookies are half-decorated with a bright and tangy passionfruit glaze, then sprinkled with more shredded coconut for a taste of the tropics. It's like a Hawaiian vacation in a cookie. *Aloha!*

Make the Dough: In a small bowl, whisk together the flour, salt, and baking powder. Set aside.

In a large mixing bowl, beat the butter and granulated sugar on medium speed until light and fluffy. Add the egg and vanilla and beat until smooth. Add the flour mixture and beat until no dry streaks remain. Add the macadamia nuts and coconut and beat until evenly distributed in the dough. Gather the dough into a ball, then flatten slightly to make a disc shape. Wrap tightly in plastic and refrigerate for at least 2 hours. Dough can keep in the fridge for up to 1 week.

Bake the Cookies: Preheat the oven to 350°F (177°C) and line one or more baking sheets with parchment paper.

Unwrap the disc of dough and place it on a lightly floured work surface. Roll the dough to a large circle about ¼ inch thick. Using a 3-inch oval cutter, cut out as many shapes as possible from the dough. Transfer the cookies to the prepared baking sheets, leaving about 1 inch of space between each one. Gather and reroll the dough scraps, then cut out the remaining cookies. Place the baking sheets in the freezer for 15 minutes; this helps the cookies keep their shape while baking.

Continued . . .

Transfer the baking sheets directly to the oven and bake for 12 to 14 minutes, until the edges of the cookies begin to turn golden and the centers no longer appear wet. If baking two pans at once, swap the positions of the pans halfway through to ensure the cookies bake evenly.

Let the cookies cool on the baking sheet for 5 minutes, then transfer to a wire rack to cool completely.

Glaze the Cookies: In a small bowl, stir together the powdered sugar and 3 tablespoons passionfruit puree until smooth and creamy, adding more passionfruit puree in increments of 1 teaspoon at a time until the glaze reaches a smooth, pourable consistency.

Spread the glaze diagonally on one half of each cookie, using the back of a knife or a small spatula as a barrier to prevent the glaze from spilling onto the other side. Sprinkle coconut over the glaze while still wet, then allow to dry fully, about 20 minutes. Enjoy!

Note: Seedless passionfruit puree is available in the frozen fruit section of many grocery stores. If using fresh passionfruit, be sure to remove the seeds before use.

½ cup (48 g) almond flour

1½ cups (180 g) all-purpose flour

1½ teaspoons ground cinnamon

¼ teaspoon baking soda

¼ teaspoon ground cardamom

¼ teaspoon ground ginger

¼ teaspoon ground nutmeg

¼ teaspoon salt

⅛ teaspoon ground cloves

1 cup (213 g) brown sugar

1 stick (113 g) unsalted butter, at room temperature

1 large egg, at room temperature

Speculaas Kruidnoten

Never judge a cookie by its size. These crunchy kruidnoten from the Netherlands are small but mighty. Made with the classic speculaas flavors of cinnamon, cardamom, ginger, nutmeg, and cloves, you'll be eating these addicting Dutch sweets by the handful. Sprinkle them on a scoop of your favorite ice cream, enjoy them with your afternoon tea . . . or just snack on them throughout the day like we often do. *Eet smakelijk!*

Make the Dough: Place the almond flour in a small skillet and set over medium-low heat. Cook until lightly golden and toasted, 5 to 7 minutes, stirring often to prevent scorching. Transfer to a heatproof bowl and let cool 5 minutes.

In a small bowl, whisk together the almond flour, all-purpose flour, cinnamon, baking soda, cardamom, ginger, nutmeg, salt, and cloves. Set aside.

In a large mixing bowl, beat the brown sugar and butter until blended. Add the egg and beat until smooth. Add the flour mixture and beat until no dry streaks remain. Transfer the dough to a small bowl, cover tightly with plastic, and refrigerate for at least 2 hours. Dough can keep in the fridge for up to 1 week.

Bake the Cookies: Preheat the oven to 350°F (177°C) and line one or more baking sheets with parchment paper.

Scoop ½ teaspoon dough into a marble-sized ball and place it on the prepared baking sheet. Repeat with the remaining dough, leaving about ½ inch of space between each ball. Bake until crisp and browned on the bottom, 15 to 18 minutes. If baking two pans at once, swap the positions of the pans halfway through to ensure the cookies bake evenly.

Let the cookies cool on the baking sheet for 5 minutes, then transfer to a wire rack to cool completely. Enjoy!

1 (14-ounce/396 g) can sweetened condensed milk

¼ cup (21 g) unsweetened cocoa powder

⅛ teaspoon salt

2 tablespoons unsalted butter

Chocolate sprinkles, for rolling (about ½ cup)

20 to 22 mini paper cupcake liners

Chocolate Brigadeiro Truffles

Chocoholics unite! These traditional Brazilian fudge balls are popular throughout the equatorial country, and for good reason. Briefly cooked on the stove—no oven required—these four-ingredient bite-size truffles are simply made with condensed milk, cocoa, butter, and salt. Chilled until smooth and creamy, then covered in chocolate sprinkles, this rich and fudgy dessert will fulfill all your chocolate fantasies. *Bom apetite!*

In a small saucepan, stir together the condensed milk, cocoa, salt, and butter. Set over medium heat and continue stirring for 10 to 12 minutes, until the mixture thickens enough that when you scrape the bottom of the pan with a spatula or spoon, the bottom remains visible for several seconds. Pour the mixture onto a heatproof plate and spread it into an even layer. Transfer the plate to the fridge to cool for 20 to 30 minutes.

Pour a generous amount of chocolate sprinkles into a shallow bowl and set aside.

To make rolling the truffles easier, first lightly rub your palms with cooking spray or neutral oil. Scoop about 1 tablespoon chocolate mixture and use your hands to roll it into a smooth ball. Then roll the ball in the bowl of sprinkles until evenly coated and place the truffle in a mini paper cupcake liner. Repeat with the remaining chocolate mixture, then transfer all the truffles to a sealed container in the fridge. Keep refrigerated until ready to serve, and enjoy!

2¼ cups (270 g) all-purpose flour

1 cup (93 g) almond flour

½ teaspoon salt

2 sticks (226 g) unsalted butter,
at room temperature

1¼ cups (141 g) powdered sugar,
plus more for dusting

1 large egg, at room temperature

1 teaspoon vanilla extract

¾ cup (250 g) seedless
raspberry jam (see note)

Note: Be sure to use seedless raspberry jam, as regular raspberry jam contains large amounts of seeds that impact the texture of the cookies. If seedless jam is unavailable, a fine-mesh strainer can be used to filter out the seeds instead.

Raspberry-Filled Spitzbuebe Hearts

All you need is love . . . and a batch of raspberry-filled heart-shaped cookies. One bite of these romantic sweets from Switzerland will bring a smile to everyone's face. Spitzbuebe are soft, buttery, and extra tender thanks to powdered sugar and almond flour mixed into the dough. They're baked until lightly golden, then filled with a spoonful of raspberry jam and garnished with a flurry of powdered sugar. Put on your apron, and make this world a more loving place, one cookie at a time. *En Guete!*

Make the Dough: In a small bowl, whisk together the all-purpose flour, almond flour, and salt. Set aside.

In a large mixing bowl, beat the butter and powdered sugar on medium speed until blended. Add the egg and vanilla and beat until smooth. Add the flour mixture and beat until no dry streaks remain. Gather the dough into a ball, then flatten slightly to make a disc shape, wrap tightly in plastic, and refrigerate for at least 2 hours. Dough can keep in the fridge for up to 1 week.

Bake the Cookies: Preheat the oven to 350°F (177°C) and line one or more baking sheets with parchment paper.

Unwrap the disc of dough and place it on a lightly floured work surface. Roll the dough to a large circle about ⅛ inch thick. The dough may crack slightly, so if this happens, gently press it back together as you roll. Using a 3-inch heart cutter, cut out as many shapes as possible from the dough. Then, using a 1-inch heart cutter, cut out the centers of half the cookies. Transfer all the cookie shapes to the prepared baking sheets, leaving about 1 inch of space between each cookie. Gather and reroll the dough scraps, then cut out the remaining cookies. Place the baking sheets in the freezer for 15 minutes; this helps the cookies keep their shape while baking.

Continued . . .

Transfer the baking sheets directly to the oven and bake for 12 to 14 minutes, until the edges of the cookies are lightly golden. If baking two pans at once, swap the positions of the pans halfway through to ensure the cookies bake evenly.

Let the cookies cool on the baking sheet for 5 minutes, then transfer to a wire rack to cool completely.

Assemble the Cookies: Separate the two cookie shapes—the whole hearts will be the base for the sandwiches, and the heart cutouts will be the tops. Dust the tops of the cutout cookies with powdered sugar and set aside.

Arrange the cookie bases with the flat side up. Spread about 2 teaspoons jam over each cookie in a smooth layer. Place the sugar-dusted cookie tops on each base to make a sandwich. Enjoy!

Makes

about
32 (2-inch)
cookies

Gluten-Free

Dairy-Free

Hibiscus Suspiro Meringues

Pretty (and tasty) in pink, these delicate meringues from Costa Rica are perfectly light and crispy. The word *suspiro* means "sigh" in Spanish, and these airy confections live up to their ethereal name. The stunning color comes from dried hibiscus flowers—no food coloring needed in this easy recipe. Inspired by the refreshing beverage *agua de jamaica*, we also add a hint of lime zest to boost the tangy flavor of pure hibiscus. Shrouded in swirls of pastel purple, these gorgeous cookies are almost too pretty to eat—almost. *¡Buen apetito!*

2 large egg whites, at room temperature

¼ teaspoon cream of tartar

Pinch of salt

½ cup (99 g) granulated sugar

1 tablespoon hibiscus powder (see note)

1 teaspoon grated lime zest

½ teaspoon vanilla extract

Note: Hibiscus powder is available online or in natural food stores. Alternatively, you can buy dried hibiscus flowers and grind them yourself in a food processor or with a mortar and pestle.

Make the Meringue: In a large mixing bowl, combine the egg whites, cream of tartar, and salt and beat using the whisk attachment on medium-low speed until foamy. Raise the speed to medium-high and continue beating until soft peaks form when the whisk is lifted. With the mixer running, slowly add the sugar about 1 tablespoon at a time, waiting about 15 seconds between each addition so the sugar can fully dissolve. Once all the sugar has been added, continue beating until stiff peaks form when the whisk is lifted, about 5 minutes. Sift in the hibiscus powder using a fine-mesh strainer, then add the lime zest and vanilla and stir gently by hand to combine.

Bake the Meringues: Preheat the oven to 200°F (93°C) and line a baking sheet with parchment paper.

Fit a piping bag with a wide star tip and scoop the meringue mixture into the bag. Pipe the mixture onto the baking sheet in small, drop-shaped kisses—note that the meringues do not spread while baking, so you only need to leave about ½ inch of space between each one.

Bake the meringues for 2 hours. Then, without opening the oven door, turn off the heat. Allow the meringues to cool in the closed oven for 30 minutes, then open the oven door a few inches and allow the meringues to finish cooling in the oven for another 30 minutes. Remove from the oven, and enjoy!

For the Cookies

1¼ cups (150 g) all-purpose flour

⅓ cup (28 g) unsweetened cocoa powder

⅛ teaspoon salt

1¾ sticks (200 g) unsalted butter, at room temperature

½ cup (99 g) granulated sugar

2 cups (60 g) cornflakes

For the Icing

1½ cups (170 g) powdered sugar

2 tablespoons unsweetened cocoa powder

1 tablespoon unsalted butter, at room temperature, cubed

1 tablespoon boiling water, plus more if needed to thin

16 to 18 walnut halves, for garnish

Chocolate Roughs (aka Afghan Biscuits)

The final stop on our cookie tour is New Zealand. Despite the recipe title, these cookies are an iconic Kiwi creation. Traditionally topped with smooth chocolate icing and garnished with a walnut half, it's no wonder why these beloved biscuits are one of the most popular cookies in New Zealand. *Kia ora!*

Make the Cookies: Preheat the oven to 350°F (177°C) and line two or more baking sheets with parchment paper.

Sift the flour, ⅓ cup cocoa powder, and salt into a medium bowl using a fine-mesh strainer to remove any lumps. Whisk to combine, and set aside.

In a large mixing bowl, beat the 1¾ sticks butter and granulated sugar until light and fluffy. Add the flour mixture and beat until no dry streaks remain. Add the cornflakes and stir by hand until evenly distributed in the dough. Scoop about 2 tablespoons dough, roll into a ball, and place on the prepared baking sheet, pressing down gently to slightly flatten it. Repeat with the remaining dough, leaving about 2 inches of space between each ball. Bake until the edges are set and the centers no longer appear wet, 12 to 15 minutes. If baking two pans at once, swap the positions of the pans halfway through to ensure the cookies bake evenly.

Let the cookies cool on the baking sheet for 5 minutes, then transfer to a wire rack to cool completely.

Make the Icing and Assemble the Cookies: Place a fine-mesh strainer over a medium bowl, then sift the powdered sugar and 2 tablespoons cocoa powder into the bowl and whisk to combine. Add the 1 tablespoon butter and 1 tablespoon boiling water and stir until smooth and creamy with a frosting-like consistency, adding more boiling water ½ teaspoon at a time until the desired consistency is reached.

Spread 1 to 2 teaspoons icing on each cookie in a generous layer, then top each one with a walnut half. The icing will dry in about 20 minutes. Enjoy!

chapter 6

a bar walks into a cookie...

What defines a cookie is a question that humans have contemplated since the beginning of time. Cookies are celebrated every day, all over the globe, regardless of their shape, size, color, or nationality. Bar cookies are a vital part of the cookie family too. Desserts unite us all in their deliciousness, bringing us closer to world peace one bite at a time, and That Takes the Cookie.

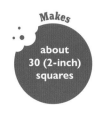

For the Crumble Topping

⅔ cup (80 g) all-purpose flour

⅓ cup (71 g) brown sugar

⅓ cup (66 g) granulated sugar

⅓ cup (38 g) finely chopped walnuts

1 tablespoon ground cinnamon

¼ teaspoon salt

6 tablespoons (85 g) cold unsalted butter, cubed

For the Blondies

2 medium Granny Smith apples

2 cups (240 g) all-purpose flour

2 teaspoons cornstarch

1 teaspoon ground cinnamon

1 teaspoon baking powder

½ teaspoon salt

¼ teaspoon ground nutmeg

2 sticks (226 g) unsalted butter, melted

1 cup (213 g) brown sugar

½ cup (99 g) granulated sugar

2 large eggs, at room temperature

2 teaspoons vanilla extract

Cinnamon Crumble Apple Blondie Bars

Just a quick word of advice: you might want to lock these away in a safe as soon as they come out of the oven. The aroma of brown sugar, cinnamon, nutmeg, and freshly baked apples will tempt even the most innocent. Imbued with the flavors of fall, these dense autumnal treats are generously filled with thinly sliced Granny Smith apples. Topped with a cinnamon sugar crumble that's brimming with chopped walnuts and tiny bits of melted butter, there's a reason these seductive squares should be kept secure.

Make the Crumble Topping: In a medium bowl, stir together the ⅔ cup flour, ⅓ cup brown sugar, ⅓ cup granulated sugar, walnuts, 1 tablespoon cinnamon, and ¼ teaspoon salt. Scatter the 6 tablespoons butter into the bowl, then use a pastry blender or two knives to cut the butter into the flour mixture until the largest pieces are the size of peas. The mixture will be dry and crumbly. Set aside.

Make the Blondies: Preheat the oven to 350°F (177°C). Lightly grease a 13 x 9-inch baking dish, then line it with a wide piece of parchment paper that covers the entire bottom of the dish and hangs over the sides by an inch or two. This creates a sling to easily lift the bars out later.

Peel and core the apples, then cut them into ⅛-inch slices about 1 inch wide. Measure 2 cups (226 g) of apple slices and set aside. Any remaining apple slices can be saved for another use.

In a medium bowl, whisk together the 2 cups flour, cornstarch, 1 teaspoon cinnamon, baking powder, ½ teaspoon salt, and nutmeg. Set aside.

In a large mixing bowl, beat the 2 sticks butter, 1 cup brown sugar, and ½ cup granulated sugar on medium speed until evenly blended. Add the eggs and vanilla and beat until smooth. Then add the flour mixture and beat until no dry streaks remain. Add the 2 cups apple slices and stir by hand until evenly distributed in the dough.

Transfer the dough to the prepared baking dish and spread into an even layer. Bake for 20 minutes, then remove the pan from the oven, place on a wire rack, and quickly sprinkle the crumble topping over the blondies in an even layer. Return the pan to the oven and continue baking for 10 to 15 minutes, until a toothpick inserted into the center comes out clean with a few crumbs sticking to it. Place the pan on a wire rack to cool completely, 60 to 75 minutes, then cover and refrigerate until chilled, at least 2 hours. Bars can keep in the fridge for up to 1 week.

Run a butter knife around the edges of the bars to loosen the sides, then use the parchment to lift the bars out of the pan. Remove the parchment and cut the bars into squares. Serve chilled or at room temperature, and enjoy!

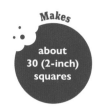

On-the-Go Blueberry Breakfast Bars

Rise and shine! Before you hit the snooze button, don't forget about the treats waiting for you in the kitchen. Those delightful breakfast bars that you baked last night are waiting for you this morning! Loaded with fresh blueberries, our on-the-go bars feature a buttery crumble made with cinnamon, oats, and grated lemon zest. Subtly sweet and filled with over a pound of fresh fruit, these sunrise saviors are here to make your mornings easy, delicious, and cooking-free!

For the Filling

4 cups (18 ounces/510 g) fresh blueberries

½ cup (99 g) granulated sugar

Juice from 1 lemon

4 teaspoons (10 g) cornstarch

1 teaspoon vanilla extract

For the Crust

2½ cups (300 g) all-purpose flour

½ cup (45 g) rolled oats

1 cup (198 g) granulated sugar

1 teaspoon baking powder

½ teaspoon ground cinnamon

¼ teaspoon salt

Grated zest from 1 lemon

2 sticks (226 g) cold unsalted butter, cubed

1 large egg

Make the Filling: In a medium bowl, combine the blueberries, ½ cup sugar, lemon juice, cornstarch, and vanilla. Toss gently to combine, and set aside.

Make the Crust: Preheat the oven to 350°F (177°C). Lightly grease a 13 x 9-inch baking dish, then line it with a wide piece of parchment paper that covers the entire bottom of the dish and hangs over the sides by an inch or two. This creates a sling to easily lift the bars out later.

In a large bowl, stir together the flour, oats, 1 cup sugar, baking powder, cinnamon, salt, and lemon zest. Scatter the butter into the bowl, then add the egg. Use a pastry blender or two knives to cut the butter into the flour mixture until the largest pieces are the size of peas. The mixture will be dry and crumbly, but it will clump together when squeezed gently.

Scatter half of the crumb mixture into the prepared baking dish and use your hands to press it into an even layer about ¼ inch thick.

Pour the blueberry mixture (including any liquid in the bowl) over the crust, spreading it into an even layer. Sprinkle the remaining crumb mixture over the blueberries in an even layer all the way to the edges.

Bake for 55 to 60 minutes, until the bars are bubbly and

lightly golden brown on top. Place the pan on a wire rack to cool completely, 60 to 75 minutes, then cover and refrigerate until chilled, at least 2 hours. Bars can keep in the fridge for up to 1 week.

Run a butter knife around the edges of the bars to loosen the sides, then use the parchment to lift the bars out of the pan. Remove the parchment and cut the bars into squares. Serve chilled or at room temperature, and enjoy!

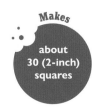

Rocky Road Chocolate Chip Cookie Bars

For the Bars

2 cups (240 g) all-purpose flour

1 teaspoon baking soda

1 teaspoon salt

2 sticks (226 g) unsalted butter, melted

1 cup (213 g) brown sugar

½ cup (99 g) granulated sugar

2 large eggs

2 teaspoons vanilla extract

2 cups (340 g) semisweet chocolate chips

1 cup (50 g) mini marshmallows (see note)

½ cup (57 g) finely chopped walnuts

For the Garnish

4 tablespoons mini marshmallows (see note)

3 tablespoons semisweet chocolate chips

3 tablespoons finely chopped walnuts

Brace yourself: this cookie combo is about to blow your mind. Crispy and golden on the outside and filled with gooey melted chocolate throughout, these bountiful bars are packed with Rocky Road realness—chocolate chips, mini marshmallows, and crunchy walnuts. Yes, they're obviously something to get excited about—just be aware of your surroundings before you scream with delight.

Preheat the oven to 350°F (177°C). Lightly grease a 13 x 9-inch baking dish, then line it with a wide piece of parchment paper that covers the entire bottom of the dish and hangs over the sides by an inch or two. This creates a sling to easily lift the bars out later.

In a medium bowl, whisk together the flour, baking soda, and salt. Set aside.

In a large mixing bowl, beat the butter, brown sugar, and granulated sugar on medium speed until evenly blended. Add the eggs and vanilla and beat until smooth. Then add the flour mixture and beat until no dry streaks remain. Add the 2 cups chocolate chips, 1 cup mini marshmallows, and ½ cup walnuts and beat until evenly distributed in the dough.

Transfer the dough to the prepared baking dish and spread into an even layer. Garnish the top with the 4 tablespoons mini marshmallows, 3 tablespoons chocolate chips, and 3 tablespoons walnuts, scattering them evenly over the surface.

Bake for 25 to 30 minutes, until a toothpick inserted into the center comes out mostly clean with a few gooey crumbs sticking to it. Place the pan on a wire rack to cool completely, 60 to 75 minutes.

Run a butter knife around the edges of the bars to loosen the sides, then use the parchment to lift the bars out of the pan. Remove the parchment and cut the bars into squares. Serve at room temperature, and enjoy!

Note: If mini marshmallows are unavailable, simply cut larger marshmallows into ½-inch pieces.

Maple Toasted Pecan Bars

Is it a pie? Is it a cookie? Is it a bar? These bewildering bites may blur the lines of cookie category, but one thing is certain—they're unquestionably delicious. If you're a pecan pie enthusiast, may we introduce the dessert of your dreams. Resting on a buttery shortbread cookie crust and filled with the warm, comforting flavors of toasted pecans and real maple syrup, these satisfying squares are in a cookie class of their own.

For the Crust

1 cup (120 g) all-purpose flour

¼ teaspoon salt

1 stick (113 g) unsalted butter, at room temperature

¼ cup (53 g) brown sugar

2 tablespoons granulated sugar

For the Filling

1½ cups (165 g) pecans

½ cup (165 g) maple syrup

½ cup (107 g) brown sugar

¼ teaspoon salt

2 large eggs, at room temperature

¼ teaspoon maple extract

Make the Crust: Preheat the oven to 350°F (177°C). Lightly grease an 8-inch square baking dish, then line it with a wide piece of parchment paper that covers the entire bottom of the dish and hangs over the sides by an inch or two. This creates a sling to easily lift the bars out later.

In a small bowl, whisk together the flour and ¼ teaspoon salt. Set aside.

In a large mixing bowl, beat the butter, ¼ cup brown sugar, and granulated sugar on medium speed until light and fluffy. Add the flour mixture and beat until no dry streaks remain.

Transfer the dough to the prepared baking dish and spread it into an even layer about ¼ inch thick. Bake for 15 minutes, then place the pan on a wire rack and set aside.

Make the Filling: Scatter the pecans in a dry skillet and place over medium heat. Cook, stirring occasionally, until toasted and fragrant, 5 to 7 minutes. Transfer to a heatproof plate and set in the freezer for 5 minutes to cool. Coarsely chop the pecans and set aside.

In a small saucepan, combine the maple syrup, ½ cup brown sugar, and ¼ teaspoon salt. Bring to a simmer over medium heat, then pour into a medium heatproof bowl and let cool until warm but no longer hot, 5 to 10 minutes. Add the eggs and maple extract and stir until blended. Add the pecans and stir until combined. Pour the mixture onto the crust and spread into an even layer.

Bake until the edges are golden and the center no longer jiggles when the pan is nudged, 25 to 30 minutes. Place the pan on a wire rack to cool completely, 60 to 75 minutes, then cover and refrigerate until chilled, at least 2 hours. Bars can keep in the fridge for up to 1 week.

Run a butter knife around the edges of the bars to loosen the sides, then use the parchment to lift the bars out of the pan. Remove the parchment and cut the bars into squares. Serve chilled or at room temperature, and enjoy!

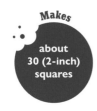

Makes about 30 (2-inch) squares

Cookies and Cream Brownie Bars with a Waffle Cone Crust

For the Crust

12 packaged waffle cones (195 g)

¼ cup (50 g) granulated sugar

6 tablespoons (85 g) unsalted butter, melted

For the Brownies

1 cup (170 g) semisweet chocolate chips

⅓ cup (57 g) chopped unsweetened chocolate (100% cacao)

1½ sticks (170 g) unsalted butter, cubed

1½ cups (297 g) granulated sugar

1 teaspoon salt

4 large eggs, at room temperature

1 tablespoon vanilla extract

1 cup (120 g) all-purpose flour

18 Oreo cookies (210 g), coarsely chopped, plus 3 more for garnish

Be careful not to drool on the page as you read this. You'll need to preserve this recipe, since you'll be making it on repeat for years to come. It all begins with the perfect chocolate brownie: rich and chewy, and chock-full of Oreos, with a cookie in every bite. Resting on a crispy waffle cone crust and sprinkled with even more Oreos on top, these fudgy brownie bars are pure chocolate decadence. If you weren't drooling before, you might want to check again.

Make the Crust: Preheat the oven to 350°F (177°C). Lightly grease a 13 x 9-inch baking dish, then line it with a wide piece of parchment paper that covers the entire bottom of the dish and hangs over the sides by an inch or two. This creates a sling to easily lift the bars out later.

Break up the waffle cones into a food processor, then pulse until coarsely ground and sandy-textured. Measure 1½ cups waffle cone crumbs and transfer to a small bowl—any remaining crumbs can be discarded or saved for another use. Add the ¼ cup sugar and 6 tablespoons butter to the crumbs and stir until blended. Pour into the prepared baking dish and use your hands or a spatula to press it into an even layer about ¼ inch thick.

Bake for 5 minutes, then place the pan on a wire rack and set aside.

Make the Brownies: Fill a small saucepan with 1 to 2 inches of water and bring to a simmer over medium heat. Place a large heatproof bowl over the pan, so the bottom of the bowl rests above the surface of the simmering water. Place the chocolate chips, unsweetened chocolate, and 1½ sticks butter in the bowl and stir until melted and smooth with no lumps remaining. Carefully remove the hot bowl

Continued . . .

from the pan and set aside to cool for 5 minutes. Then add the 1½ cups sugar and salt and stir until blended. Add the eggs one at a time, stirring until smooth between each addition. Add the vanilla and stir to combine. Then add the flour and stir until no dry streaks remain. Add the Oreos and stir until evenly distributed in the batter. Pour the batter onto the crust and spread into an even layer. Top with 3 additional Oreos.

Bake for 25 to 30 minutes, until a toothpick inserted into the center comes out clean with a few crumbs sticking to it. Place the pan on a wire rack to cool completely, 60 to 75 minutes, then cover and refrigerate until chilled, at least 2 hours. Bars can keep in the fridge for up to 1 week.

Run a butter knife around the edges of the bars to loosen the sides, then use the parchment to lift the bars out of the pan. Remove the parchment and cut the bars into squares. Serve chilled or at room temperature, and enjoy!

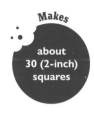

Makes about 30 (2-inch) squares

For the Banana Bread Bars

2 cups (240 g) all-purpose flour

1 teaspoon baking soda

¾ teaspoon salt

1 stick (113 g) unsalted butter, at room temperature

1½ cups (297 g) granulated sugar

2 large eggs, at room temperature

1 tablespoon gold or silver rum

2 teaspoons vanilla extract

¾ cup (170 g) sour cream

2 cups (480 g) mashed ripe bananas (about 5 to 6, see note)

1 cup (160 g) coarsely chopped semisweet chocolate

For the Frosting

¼ cup (29 g) chopped walnuts

2 sticks (226 g) unsalted butter, at room temperature

1 teaspoon vanilla extract

½ teaspoon salt

3 cups (339 g) powdered sugar

Chocolate Chunk Banana Bread Bars with Toasted Walnuts

There's only one way to make banana bread—overflowing with lots of bananas and chocolate chips. We took our favorite loaf recipe and transformed it into portable, handheld bars so you can have banana bread whenever and wherever you want. These bars are soft, moist, and exceptionally delicate; like biting into a banana-flavored cloud. Loaded with huge chunks of semisweet chocolate, they're also spiked with vanilla and a splash of rum. Garnished with smooth vanilla frosting and a sprinkle of toasted walnuts, your search for the best banana bread recipe officially ends here.

Make the Banana Bread Bars: Preheat the oven to 350°F (177°C). Lightly grease a 13 x 9-inch baking dish, then line it with a wide piece of parchment paper that covers the entire bottom of the dish and hangs over the sides by an inch or two. This creates a sling to easily lift the bars out later.

In a small bowl, whisk together the flour, baking soda, and ¾ teaspoon salt. Set aside.

In a large mixing bowl, beat the 1 stick butter and granulated sugar on medium speed until light and fluffy. Add the eggs, rum, and 2 teaspoons vanilla and beat until smooth. Add the sour cream and bananas and beat until smooth. Add the flour mixture and beat until no dry streaks remain. Add the chocolate and beat until evenly distributed in the dough.

Transfer the dough to the prepared baking dish and spread into an even layer. Bake for 30 to 35 minutes, until a toothpick inserted into the center comes out clean with a few crumbs sticking to it. Place the pan on a wire rack to cool completely, 60 to 75 minutes.

Continued . . .

Make the Frosting: Scatter the walnuts in a dry skillet and place over medium heat. Cook, stirring occasionally, until toasted and fragrant, 5 to 7 minutes. Transfer to a heatproof plate and set in the freezer for 5 minutes to cool.

In a large mixing bowl, beat the 2 sticks butter on medium speed until light and fluffy. Add the 1 teaspoon vanilla and ½ teaspoon salt and beat until smooth. Sift the powdered sugar into the bowl, then continue beating until smooth and creamy. Set aside.

Run a butter knife around the edges of the bars to loosen the sides, then use the parchment to lift the bars out of the pan. Remove the parchment.

Scoop the frosting on top of the bars, then spread into an even layer. Sprinkle the walnuts over the frosting. Cut into squares, and enjoy!

Note: When selecting ripe bananas, look for fruit that is yellow with little brown freckles, not covered in dark brown patches. Bananas that are too brown are past their prime and will negatively affect the flavor of the bars, and bananas that are green and underripe are often sour and not sweet enough.

Peanut Butter Pretzel Fudge Bars

For the Pretzel Crust

4 ounces (113 g) salted pretzels

1 tablespoon granulated sugar

5 tablespoons (71 g) unsalted butter, melted

For the Peanut Butter Fudge

1 (7-ounce/198 g) jar marshmallow crème

1 cup (198 g) granulated sugar

1 (5-ounce/147 ml) can evaporated milk

2 tablespoons unsalted butter

¼ teaspoon plus ⅛ teaspoon salt

⅔ cup (180 g) no-stir creamy peanut butter

½ teaspoon vanilla extract

Flaky sea salt, for garnish (optional)

Your favorite snack is now a dreamy dessert. If you've ever polished off a bag of peanut butter–filled pretzels in one sitting, this recipe is for you. Sweet and salty, smooth and crunchy, these addicting bars have everything. A layer of the creamiest peanut butter fudge rests on a crispy pretzel crumb crust, and each slice is topped with a pinch of flaky sea salt. No chocolate here—this is pure peanut butter pretzel perfection.

Make the Crust: Preheat the oven to 350°F (177°C). Lightly grease an 8-inch square baking dish, then line it with a wide piece of parchment paper that covers the entire bottom of the dish and hangs over the sides by an inch or two. This creates a sling to easily lift the bars out later.

Break up the pretzels into a food processor and pulse until coarsely ground and sandy-textured. Measure 1 cup crumbs and transfer to a small bowl—any remaining crumbs can be discarded or saved for another use. Add the 1 tablespoon sugar and 5 tablespoons butter to the crumbs and stir until blended. Pour into the prepared baking dish and use your hands or a spatula to press it into an even layer about ¼ inch thick. Bake for 8 minutes, then place the pan on a wire rack and set aside.

Make the Fudge: In a medium saucepan, combine the marshmallow crème, 1 cup sugar, evaporated milk, 2 table-spoons butter, and salt. Place the pan on the stove but do not turn on the heat yet.

Measure the peanut butter into a small bowl, and have the vanilla bottle and measuring spoon close by—this is because both ingredients need to be added quickly once the fudge mixture is ready.

Set the heat to medium and begin stirring the mixture with a silicone spatula. Continue stirring, scraping the sides and bottom of the pan often to prevent scorching, until the

Continued . . .

mixture begins to simmer. Once the entire surface—not just the edges—is covered with popping bubbles, start a timer for 5 minutes. If the mixture is boiling too rapidly or if you begin to see any dark spots as you stir, reduce the heat slightly. Continue to stir until the timer rings, then turn off the heat, and quickly add the peanut butter and vanilla, stirring until smooth and creamy. Immediately pour the mixture into the prepared crust, spread into an even layer, and let rest at room temperature until fully cooled, 1 to 2 hours, then cover and refrigerate until chilled, at least 2 hours. Bars can keep in the fridge for up to 1 week.

Run a butter knife around the edges of the bars to loosen the sides, then use the parchment to lift the bars out of the pan. Remove the parchment and cut into 1-inch pieces. You can lightly coat the knife with a few drops of neutral vegetable oil between cuts, if needed to prevent sticking. Garnish each square with a pinch of sea salt, if desired. Serve chilled, and enjoy!

Makes about 16 (2-inch) squares

Coconut Nanaimo Bars

Nanaimo bars are a regional Canadian specialty from the seaside town of Nanaimo on Vancouver Island. Originally created in the 1950s, this no-bake dessert is traditionally prepared in three layers: a chocolate-coconut-graham cracker crust, a custard filling in the middle, and chocolate ganache on top. There are countless flavor variations like vanilla, peanut butter, and mocha, but this version features a creamy coconut center to highlight the sweet, shredded coconut in the crust. There's no oven needed to make this recipe, just a sweet tooth and an appetite.

For the Crust

1 stick (113 g) unsalted butter, cubed

¼ cup (50 g) granulated sugar

5 tablespoons (26 g) unsweetened cocoa powder, sifted

⅛ teaspoon salt

1 large egg, at room temperature

1¾ cups (180 g) graham cracker crumbs (about 12 crackers)

1 cup (103 g) sweetened shredded coconut

½ cup (60 g) finely chopped almonds

For the Filling

1 stick (113 g) unsalted butter, at room temperature

2 tablespoons plus 2 teaspoons heavy cream

2 tablespoons instant vanilla pudding powder

¼ teaspoon salt

2 cups (226 g) powdered sugar, sifted

1½ to 2 teaspoons coconut extract

Make the Crust: Lightly grease an 8-inch square baking dish, then line it with a wide piece of parchment paper that covers the entire bottom of the dish and hangs over the sides by an inch or two. This creates a sling to easily lift the bars out later.

Fill a small saucepan with 1 to 2 inches of water and bring to a simmer over medium heat. Place a medium heatproof bowl over the pan, so the bottom of the bowl rests above the surface of the simmering water. Place the 1 stick butter, granulated sugar, cocoa powder, and ⅛ teaspoon salt in the bowl and stir until melted and smooth. Add the egg and whisk until thickened and creamy, about 3 minutes. Remove the bowl from the pan and set on a heatproof surface. Add the graham cracker crumbs, coconut, and almonds and stir until evenly blended. Transfer the mixture to the prepared baking dish and use your hands or a spatula to press it into an even layer about ½ inch thick. Place the pan in the fridge while preparing the filling.

Make the Filling: In a large mixing bowl, beat the 1 stick butter, heavy cream, pudding powder, and ¼ teaspoon salt on medium speed until evenly blended. Sift the powdered sugar into the bowl to remove any lumps, then beat until smooth. Add 1½ teaspoons coconut extract and beat to combine. Taste for coconut and add ½ teaspoon more extract,

Continued...

For the Topping

4 ounces (113 g/about ⅔ cup) chopped semisweet chocolate

2 tablespoons unsalted butter

if desired. Scoop the mixture onto the prepared crust and spread into an even layer with a smooth top. Place the pan in the fridge to chill for 15 minutes.

Make the Topping: Fill a small saucepan with 1 to 2 inches of water and bring to a simmer over medium heat. Place a small heatproof bowl over the pan, so the bottom of the bowl rests above the surface of the simmering water. Place the chocolate and 2 tablespoons butter in the bowl and stir until melted and smooth with no lumps remaining. Remove the bowl from the pan and let cool for 2 to 3 minutes. Then pour the warm chocolate mixture over the filling, spreading it into an even layer. Place the pan in the fridge to chill for 20 minutes.

Run a butter knife around the edges of the bars to loosen the sides, then use the parchment to lift the bars out of the pan. Remove the parchment and cut the bars into squares. Serve chilled, and enjoy!

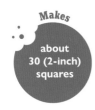

For the Crust

2 sticks (226 g) unsalted butter, at room temperature

1 cup (113 g) powdered sugar, sifted

½ teaspoon salt

2⅔ cups (320 g) all-purpose flour

For the Filling

5 cups (975 g) diced peaches (see note)

½ cup (99 g) granulated sugar

5 teaspoons cornstarch

1 tablespoon bourbon or whiskey

Grated zest from 1 lemon

2 teaspoons lemon juice

1 teaspoon ground cinnamon

½ teaspoon salt

For the Topping

1 cup (89 g) rolled oats

1 cup (213 g) brown sugar

½ cup (60 g) all-purpose flour

1½ teaspoons ground cinnamon

¼ teaspoon salt

1 stick (113 g) cold unsalted butter, cubed

Bourbon Peach Pie Bars

It's always happy hour with these bourbon peach pie bars. They have a simple shortbread crust and a filling that tastes just like peach pie. Baked with fresh peaches, lemon zest, and a splash of bourbon, these golden squares are topped with a buttery crumble made with brown sugar, oats, and cinnamon. It's five o'clock somewhere, so raise a glass (and a bar) and let's all say cheers to this gorgeous, summery handheld dessert.

Make the Crust: Preheat the oven to 350°F (177°C). Lightly grease a 13 x 9-inch baking dish, then line it with a wide piece of parchment paper that covers the entire bottom of the dish and hangs over the sides by an inch or two. This creates a sling to easily lift the bars out later.

In a large mixing bowl, beat the 2 sticks butter, powdered sugar, and ½ teaspoon salt on medium speed until light and fluffy. Add the 2⅔ cups flour and beat until no dry streaks remain.

Transfer the mixture to the prepared baking dish and use your hands or a spatula to press it into an even layer about ½ inch thick. Bake for 12 to 15 minutes, until lightly golden around the edges. Set the pan on a wire rack to cool briefly while preparing the filling and topping.

Make the Filling: In a large bowl, stir together the peaches, granulated sugar, cornstarch, bourbon, lemon zest, lemon juice, 1 teaspoon cinnamon, and ½ teaspoon salt. Toss to combine evenly and set aside.

Make the Topping: In a large mixing bowl, whisk together the oats, brown sugar, ½ cup flour, 1½ teaspoons cinnamon, and ¼ teaspoon salt until evenly blended. Scatter the 1 stick butter into the bowl, then use a pastry blender or two knives to cut the butter into the flour mixture until the largest pieces are the size of peas. Set aside.

Continued . . .

Note: If using fresh peaches, you will use about 4 to 5 peaches, depending on size. To peel them easily, simply dip them in boiling water for 30 seconds, then dip them in ice water to cool them down, and the skins will slip right off.

If using canned peaches, you will use about 4 (15-ounce) cans. For best results, look for peaches canned in juice with no added sugar.

Pour the peach filling onto the prepared crust, including any liquid in the bowl, spreading the mixture evenly in the pan. Then sprinkle the topping over the peaches in an even layer. Bake until golden and bubbly around the edges, 50 to 55 minutes. Place the pan on a wire rack to cool completely, 60 to 75 minutes.

Run a butter knife around the edges of the bars to loosen the sides, then use the parchment to lift the bars out of the pan. Remove the parchment and cut the bars into squares. Serve and enjoy!

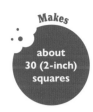

Makes about 30 (2-inch) squares

For the Crust

2 cups (208 g) graham cracker crumbs (about 14 crackers)

½ cup (99 g) granulated sugar

¼ cup (30 g) all-purpose flour

¼ teaspoon salt

1 stick (113 g) unsalted butter, melted

For the Cheesecake

24 ounces (680 g) cream cheese, at room temperature

1½ cups (297 g) granulated sugar

¼ cup (57 g) sour cream, at room temperature

1 tablespoon vanilla extract

¼ teaspoon salt

Grated zest from 1 lemon

4 large eggs, at room temperature

For the Strawberry Layer

6 ounces (170 g) fresh straw-berries, plus more for garnish

2 cups (454 g) sour cream, at room temperature

½ cup (99 g) granulated sugar

Whipped cream, for garnish (optional)

Strawberry Cheesecake Bars

You don't need a fork and knife to enjoy these strawberry cheesecake bars. Not only is this the tastiest cheesecake you'll ever try, it's also conveniently portable so you can enjoy it anytime. The vanilla center is smooth and velvety and topped with a pretty pink strawberry layer that's tangy and sweet. Capped with a fresh berry, each slice is strawberry cheesecake paradise.

Make the Crust: Preheat the oven to 300°F (149°C). Lightly grease a 13 x 9-inch baking dish, then line it with a wide piece of parchment paper that covers the entire bottom of the dish and hangs over the sides by an inch or two. This creates a sling to easily lift the bars out later.

In a large bowl, combine the graham cracker crumbs, ½ cup sugar, flour, and ¼ teaspoon salt and stir to combine. Pour in the butter and stir until evenly blended. Transfer the mixture to the prepared baking dish and use your hands or a spatula to press it into an even layer about ¼ inch thick.

Bake for 15 minutes, then set the pan on a wire rack to cool briefly while preparing the filling.

Make the Filling and Bake the Cheesecake: In a large mixing bowl, beat the cream cheese, 1½ cups sugar, ¼ cup sour cream, vanilla, ¼ teaspoon salt, and lemon zest on medium speed until smooth and blended. Add the eggs one at a time, stirring by hand between each addition. Stir by hand until the mixture is evenly blended, then pour into the prepared crust.

Bake for 40 to 45 minutes, until the edges are lightly golden and the center is set. To test for doneness, nudge the side of the pan gently; if the center ripples like liquid, it is not set yet. The center will jiggle like gelatin when fully set. Note: while the cheesecake is baking, prepare the strawberry layer.

Continued...

Make the Strawberry Layer: In a blender or food processor, blend the strawberries until pureed. Add the 2 cups sour cream and ½ cup sugar and blend until smooth and creamy.

Once the cheesecake is done, remove it from the oven, then gently pour the strawberry mixture over the top, spreading it into an even layer. Return the pan to the oven and bake for 15 to 25 minutes, until the center is set and no longer liquid. Place the pan on a wire rack to cool completely, 60 to 75 minutes, then cover and refrigerate until fully chilled and firm enough to slice, 2 to 4 hours. Slice into squares, then garnish each square with a slice of strawberry. If desired, top each square with a dollop of whipped cream before adding the strawberry slice. Serve chilled, and enjoy!

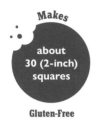

15 ounces (425 g) marshmallows

**5 tablespoons (71 g)
unsalted butter**

½ teaspoon salt

**1 cup (170 g) semisweet chocolate
chips**

**3 tablespoons bittersweet
chocolate chips (about 65% cacao)**

**1 tablespoon chopped unsweet-
ened chocolate (100% cacao)**

6 cups (166 g) crisp rice cereal

**6 tablespoons (68 g) mini
semisweet chocolate chips**

Crispy Triple Chocolate Marshmallow Treats

**Few desserts are easier to make than these crispy marsh-
mallow treats. You just stir a few ingredients on the stove,
then spread the melty marshmallow mixture in a baking
dish, let it cool, and that's it. This extra-chocolaty version
uses a trio of chocolates—bittersweet, semisweet, and
unsweetened—plus extra marshmallows to make these
crispy treats perfectly chocolaty, triply tasty, extra chewy,
and positively delicious.**

Lightly grease a 13 x 9-inch baking dish, then line it with a
wide piece of parchment paper that covers the entire bottom
of the dish and hangs over the sides by an inch or two. This
creates a sling to easily lift the bars out later.

In a large deep saucepan, combine the marshmallows, butter, and salt. Set over medium heat and cook, stirring often,
until the marshmallows melt and the mixture is smooth
with no lumps remaining. Add the semisweet chocolate
chips, bittersweet chocolate chips, and unsweetened chocolate and stir quickly until the mixture is melted and blended.
Turn off the heat, pour in the cereal, and stir until evenly
coated. Transfer the mixture to the prepared baking dish
and press into an even layer. Top with the mini chocolate
chips, gently pressing the chips onto the surface of the bars.
Let cool to room temperature, 15 to 20 minutes.

Run a butter knife around the edges of the bars to loosen the
sides, then use the parchment to lift the bars out of the pan.
Remove the parchment and cut the bars into squares. Enjoy!

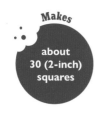

1½ cups (156 g) graham cracker crumbs (about 11 crackers)

¾ teaspoon salt

1 stick (113 g) unsalted butter, melted

1 (14-ounce/396 g) can sweetened condensed milk

2 tablespoons canned pumpkin puree

1 teaspoon ground cinnamon

1 teaspoon ground ginger

½ teaspoon ground nutmeg

¼ teaspoon ground allspice

1 cup (170 g) semisweet chocolate chips

1 cup (170 g) butterscotch chips

1 cup (120 g) finely chopped hazelnuts

1 cup (103 g) sweetened shredded coconut

Pumpkin Spice 7-Layer Bars

7-Layer Bars (also known as Magic Bars) are named for their seven luxurious layers of flavor. The base is a buttery graham cracker crust, which is topped with sweetened condensed milk, chocolate chips, butterscotch chips, chopped nuts, and shredded coconut, then baked to perfection. This cozy, fall-inspired version features crunchy hazelnuts and an aromatic pumpkin spice mixture with cinnamon, ginger, nutmeg, and allspice. These bars are easy to make, and they come together in minutes.

Preheat the oven to 350°F (177°C). Lightly grease a 13 x 9-inch baking dish, then line it with a wide piece of parchment paper that covers the entire bottom of the dish and hangs over the sides by an inch or two. This creates a sling to easily lift the bars out later.

In a medium bowl, combine the graham cracker crumbs and ¼ teaspoon of the salt and stir to combine. Pour in the butter and stir until evenly blended. Transfer the mixture to the prepared baking dish and use your hands or a spatula to press it into an even layer about ¼ inch thick.

In a medium bowl (you can use the same bowl, if desired), combine the condensed milk, pumpkin puree, cinnamon, ginger, nutmeg, allspice, and the remaining ½ teaspoon salt. Stir until blended, then pour over the crust and spread into an even layer.

In a large bowl, toss together the chocolate chips, butterscotch chips, hazelnuts, and coconut. Sprinkle handfuls of the chip mixture over the condensed milk, creating an even layer of toppings all the way to the edges of the pan. Bake for 25 minutes, then transfer to a wire rack to cool completely.

Run a butter knife around the edges of the bars to loosen the sides, then use the parchment to lift the bars out of the pan. Remove the parchment and cut the bars into squares, and enjoy!

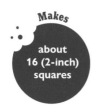

Silky Cherry-Lime Bars

If you love sour desserts, our bright and tangy cherry-lime bars will put some pep in your step. Similar to lemon bars—but even creamier—these silky squares have a smooth, custard-like lime filling made from coconut milk, lime zest, and freshly squeezed lime juice. It rests on a crispy lime-infused shortbread crust, which is topped with a thin layer of tart dried cherry puree. Served chilled and dusted with powdered sugar, these scrumptious bars make a light and refreshing after-dinner treat . . . or they can be snacked on repeatedly throughout the day. We recommend both.

For the Crust

1 stick (113 g) unsalted butter, at room temperature

¼ cup (50 g) granulated sugar

¼ cup (28 g) powdered sugar

¼ teaspoon salt

Grated zest from 1 lime

1 cup (120 g) all-purpose flour

For the Cherry Layer

1¼ cups (184 g) dried tart cherries

2 to 3 tablespoons water

For the Lime Layer

1 cup (240 g) canned coconut milk

Grated zest from 2 limes

½ cup (118 ml) lime juice (about 5 limes)

⅓ cup (66 g) granulated sugar

3 large eggs, at room temperature

3 tablespoons cornstarch

⅛ teaspoon salt

Powdered sugar, for dusting

Make the Crust: Preheat the oven to 350°F (177°C). Lightly grease an 8-inch square baking dish, then line it with a wide piece of parchment paper that covers the entire bottom of the dish and hangs over the sides by an inch or two. This creates a sling to easily lift the bars out later.

In a large mixing bowl, beat the butter, ¼ cup granulated sugar, ¼ cup powdered sugar, ¼ teaspoon salt, and zest from 1 lime on medium speed until light and fluffy. Add the flour and beat until no dry streaks remain.

Transfer the dough to the prepared baking dish and spread into an even layer. Bake for 15 to 18 minutes, until the edges are golden, then set the pan on a wire rack to cool briefly while preparing the filling.

Make the Cherry Layer: Place the cherries in a food processor or blender and pulse until finely chopped. Add 1 tablespoon water and continue to blend, scraping down the sides as needed and adding more water 1 tablespoon at a time, until the cherries form a smooth paste. Spread the paste onto the crust in a thin, even layer. Set aside.

Make the Lime Layer: When opening the can of coconut milk, note that there is a thick layer of cream at the top of the can and a layer of thinner liquid beneath. Scoop all the thick cream into a measuring cup, then add the thin liquid

Continued . . .

until it reaches 1 cup. Any remaining coconut milk can be discarded or saved for another use.

In a blender, combine the 1 cup coconut milk with the zest from 2 limes, lime juice, ⅓ cup granulated sugar, eggs, cornstarch, and ⅛ teaspoon salt. Blend until smooth, then pour over the cherry layer.

Bake for 35 to 45 minutes, until the center is set. To test for doneness, nudge the side of the pan gently; if the center ripples like liquid, it is not set yet. The center will jiggle like gelatin when fully set.

Place the pan on a wire rack to cool completely, about 60 minutes, then cover and refrigerate until fully chilled, 2 to 4 hours.

Run a butter knife around the edges of the bars to loosen the sides, then use the parchment to lift the bars out of the pan. Remove the parchment and cut the bars into squares, then dust each square with a generous layer of powdered sugar. Serve chilled, and enjoy!

The original

NET WT 5 OZ (141 g)

chapter 7

cookie mash-ups

This chapter is a hats-off to mash-ups. We took all your favorite desserts and transformed them into timeless cookie creations. You'll thank us once you bake Sticky Toffee Pudding Cookies (page 234) for the first time, or when you bite into our heavenly Tiramisu Cloud Cookies (page 268). In this chapter, you get two treats in the bite of one, and That Takes the Cookie.

1¼ cups (150 g) all-purpose flour

½ teaspoon baking soda

½ teaspoon salt

¼ teaspoon baking powder

1 stick (113 g) unsalted butter,
at room temperature

½ cup (107 g) brown sugar

½ cup (99 g) granulated sugar

1 large egg, at room temperature

1 teaspoon vanilla extract

2 cups (15 g) popped butter-
flavored microwave popcorn,
plus more for garnish

1 cup (215 g) M&M's or other
small candy-shell chocolates

½ cup (85 g) semisweet
chocolate chips

½ cup (25 g) miniature salted
pretzels

Movie Night Cookies

Level up your next movie night with these cinematic snacks. Enjoy all your favorite concessions combined into one blockbuster dessert. Starring a fabulous cast of flavors—buttery popcorn, colorful M&M's, crunchy pretzels, and lots of chocolate chips—these copious cookies are the perfect sweet and salty accompaniment to any late-night double feature picture show. Dim the lights, pass the cookies, and let the festivities commence.

Make the Dough: In a small bowl, whisk together the flour, baking soda, salt, and baking powder. Set aside.

In a large mixing bowl, beat the butter, brown sugar, and granulated sugar on medium speed until light and fluffy. Add the egg and vanilla and beat until smooth. Add the flour mixture and beat until no dry streaks remain. Add the popcorn, M&M's, chocolate chips, and pretzels and stir by hand until evenly distributed in the dough. Cover the bowl with plastic and refrigerate for at least 2 hours. Dough can keep in the fridge for up to 1 week.

Bake the Cookies: Preheat the oven to 350°F (177°C) and line one or more baking sheets with parchment paper.

Scoop about 1½ tablespoons dough into a ball shape, adding 3 to 4 pieces of popcorn and pressing them into the dough as you form the ball. Place the ball on the prepared baking sheet and repeat with the remaining dough, leaving 2 inches of space between each one.

Bake until the edges are lightly golden and the centers no longer appear wet, 10 to 12 minutes. If baking two pans at once, swap the positions of the pans halfway through to ensure the cookies bake evenly.

Let the cookies cool on the baking sheet for 5 minutes, then transfer to a wire rack to cool completely. Enjoy!

Makes about 24 (2-inch) cookies

Sticky Toffee Pudding Cookies

Sticky toffee pudding is a classic British dessert: a light and fluffy sponge cake made with finely chopped dates, covered in toffee sauce, and often served warm with vanilla ice cream. And with this posh recipe, you can enjoy a miniature version in the form of a cookie! Flavored with cinnamon, ginger, cloves, and brown sugar, these chewy treats are coated in a caramel toffee sauce, just like the original. No forks needed here—just some napkins, since these sticky treats live up to their delectable name.

For the Cookies

6 ounces (170 g/about 1 cup) pitted dates

2 cups (240 g) all-purpose flour

1 teaspoon baking powder

½ teaspoon salt

½ teaspoon ground ginger

¼ teaspoon ground cinnamon

⅛ teaspoon ground cloves

1 stick (113 g) unsalted butter, at room temperature

½ cup (107 g) brown sugar

½ cup (99 g) granulated sugar

1 large egg, at room temperature

1 teaspoon vanilla extract

For the Toffee Sauce

1 cup (198 g) granulated sugar

3 tablespoons water

2 tablespoons light corn syrup

½ cup (118 ml) heavy cream

2 tablespoons unsalted butter, cubed

1 teaspoon vanilla extract

¼ teaspoon salt

Make the Dough: Place the dates in a heatproof bowl or measuring cup and pour in boiling water until the fruit is completely covered. Let rest for 10 minutes, then pour into a strainer to drain off the water. Chop the dates finely until the mixture becomes a chunky paste. Set aside.

In a medium bowl, whisk together the flour, baking powder, ½ teaspoon salt, ginger, cinnamon, and cloves. Set aside.

In a large mixing bowl, beat the 1 stick butter, brown sugar, and ½ cup granulated sugar on medium speed until light and fluffy. Add the egg, 1 teaspoon vanilla, and dates and beat until smooth. Add the flour mixture and beat until no dry streaks remain. Cover the bowl with plastic and refrigerate for at least 2 hours. Dough can keep in the fridge for up to 1 week.

Make the Toffee Sauce: In a small saucepan, combine the 1 cup granulated sugar, water, and corn syrup. Set over medium heat and cook, stirring often, until amber-colored, 8 to 10 minutes. Remove from the heat and add the heavy cream, 2 tablespoons butter, 1 teaspoon vanilla, and ¼ teaspoon salt carefully, as the mixture will steam vigorously. Stir until smooth and blended, then transfer to a small heatproof bowl to cool to room temperature. The toffee sauce can be made ahead and will stay fresh in the fridge for up to 1 week.

Continued . . .

234 That Takes the Cookie

Bake the Cookies: Preheat the oven to 350°F (177°C) and line one or more baking sheets with parchment paper.

Scoop about 1½ tablespoons dough into a ball and place it on the prepared baking sheet. Repeat with the remaining dough, leaving 2 inches of space between each one and placing approximately 12 dough balls per sheet.

Bake until the edges are lightly golden and the centers no longer appear wet, 10 to 12 minutes. If baking two pans at once, swap the positions of the pans halfway through to ensure the cookies bake evenly.

Let the cookies cool on the baking sheet for 5 minutes, then transfer to a wire rack to cool completely.

Glaze the Cookies: To glaze the cookies, the sauce needs to be soft enough to drizzle with a spoon, so if it is too thick, heat it for a few seconds in the microwave and stir until warm and softened.

Place one of the cookies on a fork or slotted spoon and hold it above the bowl of toffee sauce. Spoon a generous tablespoon of sauce over the cookie, coating the top completely and allowing the excess to drip back into the bowl. Transfer the cookie to a wire rack to dry, then repeat with the remaining cookies. The toffee sauce will set in about 20 minutes, although it will remain sticky. Enjoy!

For the Cookies

1½ cups (156 g) graham cracker crumbs (about 11 crackers)

1 cup (120 g) all-purpose flour

1¼ teaspoons baking soda

½ teaspoon baking powder

½ teaspoon salt

1 cup (198 g) granulated sugar

1 stick (113 g) unsalted butter, at room temperature

1 large egg, at room temperature

⅔ cup (158 ml) buttermilk, at room temperature

For the Lime Curd

¼ cup (50 g) granulated sugar

2 large eggs

1 large egg yolk

Grated zest from 2 limes

¼ cup (60 ml) lime juice

⅛ teaspoon salt

1 tablespoon unsalted butter, cubed

Key Lime Pie Whoopie Pies

You get two pies for the price of one with this glorious dessert: key lime pie plus whoopie pie equals pie squared deliciousness. Here, two soft and puffy graham cracker–flavored cookies are sandwiched together with a velvety key lime filling. These tart treats are light and summery and taste just like key lime pie. The smooth marshmallow crème filling is bright and tangy with freshly squeezed lime juice, and the cookies are buttery like a graham cracker crust. As soon as you taste one, you'll be shouting whoopie—if you haven't done so already.

Make the Dough: In a small bowl, whisk together the graham cracker crumbs, flour, baking soda, baking powder, and ½ teaspoon salt. Set aside.

In a large mixing bowl, beat the 1 cup granulated sugar and 1 stick butter on medium speed until light and fluffy. Add the egg and beat until smooth. Then add the buttermilk and beat until evenly blended. Add the flour mixture and beat until no dry streaks remain—note that the dough may appear to separate at first, but continue beating and it will blend evenly. Cover the bowl with plastic and refrigerate for at least 2 hours. Dough can keep in the fridge for up to 1 week.

Make the Lime Curd: Fill a small saucepan with 1 to 2 inches of water, and bring to a simmer over medium heat. Place a medium heatproof bowl over the pan, so the bottom of the bowl rests above the surface of the simmering water. Place the ¼ cup granulated sugar, 2 eggs, egg yolk, lime zest, lime juice, and ⅛ teaspoon salt in the bowl and whisk to combine. Continue to cook, stirring often, until the curd has thickened and the temperature reaches 170°F (77°C) on a cooking thermometer, 10 to 15 minutes.

Remove the bowl from the heat and add the 1 tablespoon butter, stirring until the butter melts and the mixture is smooth and blended. Set a fine-mesh strainer over a

Continued . . .

For Assembly

2 sticks (226 g) unsalted butter, at room temperature

1 cup (113 g) powdered sugar, sifted

1 (7-ounce/198 g) jar marshmallow crème

⅛ teaspoon salt

medium heatproof bowl and strain the curd into the bowl, removing and discarding any solids. Cover the bowl with plastic, pressing the wrap directly onto the surface of the curd to prevent a skin from forming, and refrigerate until cool, at least 2 hours. Curd can keep in the fridge for up to 1 week.

Bake the Cookies: Preheat the oven to 350°F (177°C) and line one or more baking sheets with parchment paper.

Scoop about 1½ tablespoons dough into a ball and place it on the prepared baking sheet. Repeat with the remaining dough, leaving 2 inches of space between each one and placing approximately 12 dough balls per sheet.

Bake for 8 to 10 minutes, until the edges are lightly golden and the centers no longer appear wet. If baking two pans at once, swap the positions of the pans halfway through to ensure the cookies bake evenly.

Let the cookies cool on the baking sheet for 5 minutes, then transfer to a wire rack to cool completely.

Assemble the Cookies: In a large mixing bowl, beat the 2 sticks butter and powdered sugar on medium speed until light and fluffy. Add the marshmallow crème and ⅛ teaspoon salt and beat until smooth. Add the lime curd and beat until smooth and blended.

Place one of the cookies flat side up on a piece of parchment. Spread 2 tablespoons filling onto the cookie in an even layer, then top with a second cookie to make a sandwich. Repeat with the remaining cookies and filling, and enjoy!

For the Cookies

2½ cups (300 g) all-purpose flour

½ cup (42 g) unsweetened cocoa powder, sifted

2 teaspoons ground cinnamon

2 teaspoons cream of tartar

1 teaspoon baking soda

½ teaspoon salt

1½ cups (297 g) granulated sugar

2 sticks (226 g) unsalted butter, at room temperature

2 large eggs, at room temperature

2 teaspoons vanilla extract

For the Cinnamon-Sugar

¼ cup (50 g) granulated sugar, for rolling

1 tablespoon ground cinnamon, for rolling

Mexican Hot Chocolate Snickerdoodles

The next time it's cold and rainy outside, stay inside and whip up a batch of these cozy, chocolate cinnamon snickerdoodle cookies. Inspired by the warm and comforting flavors of Mexican hot chocolate, combined with the classic chewiness of a snickerdoodle, these soft and tender cookies are rich and fudgy with a crackly top. Filled with chocolate cinnamon flavor and rolled in sparkling cinnamon-sugar, they will instantly turn gray clouds into sunny skies.

Make the Dough: In a medium bowl, whisk together the flour, cocoa powder, 2 teaspoons cinnamon, cream of tartar, baking soda, and salt. Set aside.

In a large mixing bowl, beat the 1½ cups sugar and butter on medium speed until light and fluffy. Add the eggs and vanilla and beat until smooth. Add the flour mixture and beat until no dry streaks remain. Cover the bowl with plastic and refrigerate for at least 2 hours. Dough can keep in the fridge for up to 1 week.

Bake the Cookies: Preheat oven to 350°F (177°C) and line one or more baking sheets with parchment paper. In a small bowl, stir together the ¼ cup sugar and 1 tablespoon cinnamon until blended. Set aside.

Scoop about 1½ tablespoons dough into a ball and roll it in the cinnamon-sugar mixture until evenly coated. Place the ball on the prepared baking sheet, then repeat with the remaining dough, leaving about 2 inches of space between each one and placing approximately 12 balls per sheet.

Bake for 8 to 10 minutes, until the edges of the cookies begin to darken slightly and the centers no longer appear wet. If baking two pans at once, swap the positions of the pans halfway through to ensure the cookies bake evenly.

Let the cookies cool on the baking sheet for 5 minutes, then transfer to a wire rack to cool completely. Enjoy!

Cannoli Cookie Cups

Impress the guests at your next party with a tray of cute cannoli cookie cups. These mini bite-size desserts are a light and easy way to enjoy cannoli, since they're baked, not fried. Thin, crisp cookie cups are topped with traditional Italian cannoli filling: smooth ricotta swirled with a hint of cinnamon, lemon zest, and vanilla. Garnished with mini chocolate chips and finely chopped pistachios, they're the perfect addition to any party platter.

For the Cannoli Cups

2 cups (240 g) all-purpose flour

¼ cup (50 g) granulated sugar

¼ teaspoon salt

3 tablespoons unsalted butter, at room temperature, cubed

1 large egg, at room temperature

⅓ cup (79 ml) sweet marsala wine (see note)

For the Filling

2 cups (454 g) ricotta cheese

1½ cups (170 g) powdered sugar, sifted

1 teaspoon grated lemon zest

½ teaspoon ground cinnamon

1 teaspoon vanilla extract

Mini semisweet chocolate chips, for garnish

Finely chopped pistachios, for garnish

Note: If sweet marsala wine is unavailable, you can substitute sweet vermouth or sherry, or grape juice for a nonalcoholic version.

Make the Dough: In a medium bowl, whisk together the flour, granulated sugar, and salt. Add the butter and use your fingers to blend it into the flour until sandy-textured. Add the egg and wine, stir to combine, then knead with your hands briefly until evenly blended and smooth. Gather the dough into a ball, then flatten slightly to make a disc shape. Wrap tightly in plastic and refrigerate for at least 2 hours. Dough can keep in the fridge for up to 1 week.

Make the Filling: First, drain the ricotta to prevent the filling from becoming watery. To do this, place a fine-mesh strainer over a large bowl. Line the strainer with either cheesecloth or a nut milk bag and pour in the ricotta cheese. Gather the cloth and gently squeeze the ricotta to release all the excess liquid into the bowl. If cheesecloth is unavailable, you can also use a few layers of strong paper towels, but do not squeeze too tightly, as the paper can tear.

Place the ricotta in a medium bowl, then add the powdered sugar, lemon zest, cinnamon, and vanilla and stir until blended. Keep refrigerated until ready to use, up to 2 days.

Bake the Cookies: Preheat the oven to 400°F (204°C).

Unwrap the disc of dough and place it on a lightly floured work surface. Roll the dough to a large circle about ⅛ inch thick. Using a 2½-inch circle cutter, cut out as many circles as possible from the dough. Transfer the circles to a mini cupcake pan, pressing them gently into the bottom and sides to create cup shapes. Gather and reroll the dough scraps, then cut out the remaining circles and press them into the pan.

Bake until the cookies are lightly golden, 9 to 11 minutes. Let the cookies cool in the pan for 5 minutes, then transfer to a wire rack to cool completely.

Assemble the Cookies: Spoon about 1 tablespoon ricotta filling into each cannoli cup. Garnish with chocolate chips or pistachios and serve. Enjoy!

For the Cookies

1 cup (237 ml) water

1 stick (113 g) unsalted butter

2 tablespoons brown sugar

¼ teaspoon salt

1 cup (120 g) all-purpose flour

2 large eggs, at room temperature

1 teaspoon vanilla extract

For the Cinnamon-Sugar

½ cup (99 g) granulated sugar

1 tablespoon ground cinnamon

⅛ teaspoon salt

4 tablespoons (57 g) unsalted
butter, melted, for brushing

Cinnamon Sugar Churro Cookies

If you like churros, you're going to fall in love with churro cookies. This popular fairground favorite is usually deep-fried in hot oil, but in this easy recipe, they are baked to perfection and just as addictive. Light, airy, soft, and buttery, these mini churro pillows are subtly crunchy on the outside and irresistibly tender in the middle. Rolled in cinnamon-sugar and enjoyed warm from the oven, you'll never have to wait in line for churros again.

Make the Dough: In a small saucepan, combine the water, 1 stick butter, brown sugar, and ¼ teaspoon salt. Place over medium heat and stir until the butter melts. As soon as the mixture begins to boil, add all the flour at once and stir vigorously until the dough forms a ball that pulls away from the sides of the pan, about 1 minute. Remove from the heat and transfer the dough to a large mixing bowl. Use an electric mixer to beat the dough until it is warm but no longer hot to the touch. With the mixer running, add the eggs one at a time, beating until blended between each addition. Add the vanilla, then continue beating for 2 to 3 more minutes, until smooth and glossy. The dough will still be slightly warm.

Bake the Cookies: Preheat the oven to 350°F (177°C) and line a baking sheet with parchment paper. Prepare a piping bag with a wide star tip.

Transfer the dough to the piping bag. Pipe a 3-inch line of dough onto the prepared baking sheet, using scissors to cut it off cleanly. Repeat with the remaining dough, leaving ½ inch of space between each cookie, since they do not spread much while baking.

Bake for 20 minutes, then flip the churros over and continue baking for 15 to 20 minutes until deeply golden brown. Note—if they look pale or just lightly golden, they are not done yet.

Continued . . .

Assemble the Cookies: While the churros are baking, stir together the granulated sugar, cinnamon, and ⅛ teaspoon salt in a small, wide bowl.

When the churros are done baking, remove the sheet from the oven. Immediately, brush one of the churros with butter, covering all sides, then dip it in the bowl of cinnamon-sugar until evenly coated. Place on a wire rack, then repeat with the remaining churros. Serve warm, and enjoy!

Glazed Stollen Cookies with Marzipan

They're not stolen cookies—they're Stollen cookies! Stollen (pronounced "shtollen") is a festive German Christmas bread made with rum-soaked dried fruit and spices, filled with a generous layer of marzipan, and topped with sweet vanilla icing. These colorful cookies have all the flavors of the original loaves baked into one tiny handheld treat—even the rum. Yes, they may be tempting, but there's no need to steal these Stollen cookies; this recipe makes plenty to share.

For the Cookies

3 tablespoons dried currants

3 tablespoons raisins

3 tablespoons golden raisins

3 tablespoons chopped maraschino cherries

1½ tablespoons finely chopped walnuts

2 teaspoons grated orange zest

2 teaspoons gold or silver rum

1 teaspoon orange juice

1¾ cups (210 g) all-purpose flour

½ teaspoon cream of tartar

½ teaspoon salt

½ teaspoon ground nutmeg

¼ teaspoon ground cinnamon

¼ teaspoon baking soda

1 cup (198 g) granulated sugar

1½ sticks (170 g) unsalted butter, at room temperature

1 large egg, at room temperature

1 teaspoon vanilla extract

Make the Dough: In a small bowl, stir together the currants, raisins, golden raisins, maraschino cherries, walnuts, orange zest, rum, and orange juice. Toss to combine, then let rest at room temperature for 15 minutes.

In a small bowl, whisk together the all-purpose flour, cream of tartar, salt, nutmeg, cinnamon, and baking soda. Set aside.

In a large mixing bowl, beat the 1 cup granulated sugar and butter on medium speed until light and fluffy. Add the egg and 1 teaspoon vanilla and beat until smooth. Then add the flour mixture and beat until no dry streaks remain. Add the soaked fruit mixture along with any liquid in the bowl and beat until evenly distributed in the dough. Cover the bowl with plastic and refrigerate for at least 2 hours. Dough can keep in the fridge for up to 1 week.

Make the Marzipan: In a food processor, combine the almond flour, ½ cup plus 2 tablespoons powdered sugar, and 3 tablespoons plus 2 teaspoons granulated sugar and pulse until evenly blended. Add the corn syrup and almond extract and pulse until the mixture begins to clump together. To reach a spreadable consistency, add water 1 teaspoon at a time, as needed, up to a total of 2 tablespoons. Transfer the

Continued . . .

For the Marzipan

1 cup plus 3 tablespoons (110 g) almond flour

½ cup plus 2 tablespoons (70 g) powdered sugar

3 tablespoons plus 2 teaspoons granulated sugar

2 tablespoons light corn syrup

1½ teaspoons almond extract

For the Glaze

1 cup (113 g) powdered sugar

3½ teaspoons milk of your choice

½ teaspoon vanilla extract

Note: If desired, use store-bought marzipan to save time.

marzipan to a small bowl, then cover and refrigerate if not using right away. The marzipan will stay fresh for up to a week in the fridge—note that the marzipan thickens when refrigerated, so it must be brought to room temperature for a spreadable consistency before use.

Bake the Cookies: Preheat the oven to 350°F (177°C) and line one or more baking sheets with parchment paper.

Scoop about 1½ tablespoons dough into a ball and place it on the prepared baking sheet. Repeat with the remaining dough, leaving 2 inches of space between each one.

Bake for 12 to 14 minutes, until the edges are lightly golden and the centers no longer appear wet. If baking two pans at once, swap the positions of the pans halfway through to ensure the cookies bake evenly.

Let the cookies cool on the baking sheet for 5 minutes, then transfer to a wire rack to cool completely.

Glaze the Cookies: In a small bowl, stir together the 1 cup powdered sugar, milk, and ½ teaspoon vanilla until smooth and creamy. If needed, add more milk a few drops at a time and stir until blended.

Place one cookie flat side up and spread 2 to 3 teaspoons of marzipan over it in an even layer. Place a second cookie flat side down on top to make a sandwich. Drizzle the top with the vanilla glaze and place on a wire rack to dry. Repeat with the remaining cookies, and enjoy!

⅓ cup (79 ml) warm water

8 tablespoons (99 g)
granulated sugar

2¼ teaspoons active dry yeast

2 cups (240 g) all-purpose flour

½ teaspoon salt

2 teaspoons vanilla extract

1 teaspoon maple extract

3 large eggs, at room temperature

2 sticks (226 g) unsalted butter,
at room temperature

1 cup (160 g) pearl sugar
(see note)

Powdered sugar, for dusting

Maple-Butter Belgian Waffle Cookies

What's the best way to show someone how much you care? By waking them up with a plate of freshly baked waffle cookies. Imagine their face when they bite into a warm and crisp, caramelized cookie first thing in the morning. Filled with rich maple flavor and tiny pockets of melted pearl sugar, these golden buttery treats are prepared in a waffle iron—no oven needed—and garnished with a light dusting of powdered sugar. Your special someone will thank you; just don't get any crumbs in the bed.

Make the Dough: Pour the warm water into a small bowl or measuring cup. The water should feel warm but not hot, around 105° to 110°F (40° to 44°C). Add 3 tablespoons (37 g) of the granulated sugar and stir to dissolve. Add the yeast and stir to combine. Let the mixture rest until the yeast becomes foamy, 5 to 10 minutes.

In a large mixing bowl, combine the flour, salt, and remaining 5 tablespoons (62 g) granulated sugar. Pour in the yeast mixture, then add the vanilla and maple extract and beat on low speed until combined. With the mixer running, add the eggs one at a time, beating between each addition. Then add the butter 1 tablespoon at a time, beating between each addition. Once all the butter has been added, continue beating for another 1 to 2 minutes until smooth and glossy. Cover the bowl with a damp kitchen towel and let rise until doubled in size, 1½ to 2 hours.

Once the dough has risen, add the pearl sugar and stir gently to combine. Let the dough rest for 15 minutes.

Make the Cookies: Preheat a waffle iron according to the manufacturer's instructions. If needed, lightly coat the iron with cooking spray to prevent sticking.

Using 2 tablespoons dough per cookie, place one scoop of dough in the center of each section of the waffle iron.

Continued . . .

Close the lid and cook until deeply golden, 3 to 4 minutes depending on the iron. Transfer the finished cookies to a wire rack to cool for 2 to 3 minutes. Serve warm or at room temperature and dust the cookies with powdered sugar just before serving. Enjoy!

Makes

32 to 34 (3-inch) cookies

Gluten-Free

Dairy-Free

3 cups (339 g) powdered sugar

⅔ cup (56 g) unsweetened cocoa powder

¼ teaspoon salt

3 large eggs, at room temperature

2 teaspoons vanilla extract

1½ cups (255 g) semisweet chocolate chips

Flourless Chocolate Cake Cookies

Attention chocolate lovers! These rich, chewy, and intensely chocolaty flourless chocolate cake cookies couldn't be easier to make. You mix six simple ingredients—sugar, cocoa, eggs, salt, vanilla, and chocolate chips—together in a bowl, spoon the batter onto a cookie sheet, then bake, and that's it. They come out of the oven with crisp edges and gooey chocolaty centers, and since they have no dairy or gluten, practically everyone can enjoy them. Dense, dark, and fudgy, these cookies are pure chocolate indulgence.

Make the Dough: Line one or more baking sheets with parchment paper, then lightly grease the paper with butter or cooking spray.

Sift the powdered sugar, cocoa powder, and salt into a large bowl and whisk to combine. Add the eggs and vanilla and stir until smooth and blended. Add the chocolate chips and stir to combine.

Scoop 1 tablespoon dough onto the prepared baking sheet in a small mound. Repeat with the remaining dough, leaving about 3 inches of space between each one and placing about 12 cookies per sheet. Let the dough rest on the sheets at room temperature for 30 minutes.

Bake the Cookies: Preheat the oven to 350°F (177°C).

Bake for 9 to 11 minutes, until the edges are set and the centers look slightly underdone. Let the cookies cool completely on the baking sheets, about 20 minutes, before transferring to a wire rack, since they are soft and fragile when warm. Enjoy!

Crème Brûlée Cookies

Dreams do come true. We transformed one of the most elegant desserts in French cuisine into an unforgettable cookie. It's delicately soft and tender and baked with a full tablespoon of vanilla extract. Spread on top is a layer of silky vanilla custard, crowned with a thin, crunchy lid of caramelized sugar, torched until bubbly and golden. So, what are you waiting for? Light some candles, prepare a romantic dinner, and serve these crème brûlée–inspired treats for a sweet night you'll always remember.

For the Cookies

2 cups (240 g) all-purpose flour

2 teaspoons cornstarch

½ teaspoon baking powder

¼ teaspoon baking soda

¼ teaspoon salt

1¼ cups (248 g) granulated sugar

1⅓ sticks (151 g) unsalted butter, at room temperature

2 tablespoons neutral vegetable oil

2 large eggs, at room temperature

1 tablespoon vanilla extract

For the Cream

4 large egg yolks

½ cup (99 g) granulated sugar, plus more for topping

¼ cup (28 g) cornstarch

¼ teaspoon salt

2 cups (473 ml) milk of your choice

2 tablespoons unsalted butter, cubed

1 tablespoon vanilla extract

Make the Dough: In a small bowl, whisk together the flour, 2 teaspoons cornstarch, baking powder, baking soda, and ¼ teaspoon salt. Set aside.

In a large mixing bowl, beat the 1¼ cups sugar and 1⅓ sticks butter on medium speed until light and fluffy. Add the oil, 2 eggs, and 1 tablespoon vanilla and beat until smooth. Then add the flour mixture and beat until no dry streaks remain. Cover the bowl with plastic and refrigerate for at least 2 hours. Dough can keep in the fridge for up to 1 week.

Make the Cream: In a medium bowl, whisk together the 4 egg yolks, ½ cup sugar, ¼ cup cornstarch, and ¼ teaspoon salt until smooth and blended. Set aside.

In a medium saucepan, bring the milk to a simmer over medium heat. As soon as it begins to simmer, remove the pan from the heat. While whisking constantly, add the milk to the bowl of egg yolks in a slow, steady stream—this prevents the eggs from scrambling. Once all the milk has been added, pour the mixture back into the saucepan. Continue to cook, whisking constantly, until the mixture thickens, 2 to 4 minutes. Once bubbles begin to form (you may need to stop whisking to see if the mixture is bubbling), continue cooking for 1 minute, then remove from the heat. Add the 2 tablespoons butter and 1 tablespoon vanilla and stir until melted and smooth.

Set a fine-mesh strainer over a medium heatproof bowl and strain the cream into the bowl, removing and discarding

Continued . . .

any solids. Cover the bowl with plastic, pressing the wrap directly onto the surface of the cream to prevent a skin from forming, and refrigerate until cool, at least 2 hours. Cream can keep in the fridge for up to 3 days.

Bake the Cookies: Preheat the oven to 350°F (177°C) and line one or more baking sheets with parchment paper.

Scoop about 1½ tablespoons dough into a ball and place it on the prepared baking sheet. Repeat with the remaining dough, leaving 2 inches of space between each one.

Bake for 9 to 11 minutes, until the edges are lightly golden and the centers no longer appear wet. If baking two pans at once, swap the positions of the pans halfway through to ensure the cookies bake evenly.

Let the cookies cool on the baking sheet for 5 minutes, then transfer to a wire rack to cool completely.

Assemble the Cookies: Spread about 1 tablespoon cream on one of the cookies. Sprinkle with ¼ to ½ teaspoon sugar, then use a kitchen torch to melt and caramelize the sugar until golden brown and bubbly. Repeat with the remaining cookies, and enjoy!

Makes

28 to 30
(2-inch)
cookies

Banana Pudding Bites

Alert the press: banana pudding has just been turned into a cookie. The dreamy Southern dessert known for its trifle-like layers of custard, bananas, and wafer cookies can now be enjoyed in one satisfying bite. A soft, vanilla wafer–inspired cookie is the foundation for this new revelation. It's topped with a spoonful of rich banana custard and garnished with a fresh banana slice, a dollop of whipped cream, and vanilla wafer cookie crumbles. You can't believe everything you read, so you'll just have to make them yourself to see what all the excitement is about.

For the Cookies

1½ cups (180 g) all-purpose flour

1 teaspoon cream of tartar

½ teaspoon baking soda

¼ teaspoon plus ⅛ teaspoon salt

¾ cup (149 g) granulated sugar

1 stick (113 g) unsalted butter, at room temperature

1 large egg, at room temperature

1 tablespoon vanilla extract

For the Banana Cream

4 large eggs

¾ cup (200 g) mashed bananas (about 2 to 3)

½ cup (99 g) granulated sugar

6 tablespoons (42 g) cornstarch

½ teaspoon salt

2 cups (473 ml) milk of your choice

2 tablespoons unsalted butter, cubed

1 tablespoon vanilla extract

Make the Dough: In a small bowl, whisk together the flour, cream of tartar, baking soda, and ¼ teaspoon plus ⅛ teaspoon salt. Set aside.

In a large mixing bowl, beat the ¾ cup sugar and 1 stick butter on medium speed until light and fluffy. Add the egg and 1 tablespoon vanilla and beat until smooth. Then add the flour mixture and beat until no dry streaks remain. Cover the bowl with plastic and refrigerate for at least 2 hours. Dough can keep in the fridge for up to 1 week.

Make the Banana Cream: In a medium bowl, whisk together the 4 eggs, bananas, ½ cup sugar, cornstarch, and ½ teaspoon salt until smooth and blended. Set aside.

In a medium saucepan, bring the milk to a simmer over medium heat. As soon as it begins to simmer, remove the pan from the heat. While whisking constantly, add the milk to the bowl of eggs in a slow, steady stream—this prevents the eggs from scrambling. Once all the milk has been added, pour the mixture back into the saucepan. Continue to cook, whisking constantly, until the mixture thickens, 2 to 4 minutes. Once bubbles begin to form (you may need to stop whisking to see if the mixture is bubbling), continue cooking for 1 minute, then remove from the heat. Add the 2 tablespoons butter and 1 tablespoon vanilla and stir until melted and smooth.

Continued . . .

For the Garnish

Banana slices

Crumbled vanilla wafer cookies (such as Nilla Wafers)

Whipped cream

> **Note:** The banana slices should be added just before serving, as they will turn brown fairly quickly.

Set a fine-mesh strainer over a medium heatproof bowl and strain the cream into the bowl, removing and discarding any solids. Cover the bowl with plastic, pressing the wrap directly onto the surface of the cream to prevent a skin from forming, and refrigerate until cool, at least 2 hours. Cream can keep in the fridge for up to 3 days.

Bake the Cookies: Preheat the oven to 350°F (177°C) and line one or more baking sheets with parchment paper.

Scoop 1 tablespoon dough into a ball and place it on the prepared baking sheet. Repeat with the remaining dough, leaving 2 inches of space between each one.

Bake for 8 to 10 minutes, until the edges are lightly golden and the centers no longer appear wet. If baking two pans at once, swap the positions of the pans halfway through to ensure the cookies bake evenly.

Let the cookies cool on the baking sheet for 5 minutes, then transfer to a wire rack to cool completely.

Assemble the Cookies: Spread about 1 tablespoon banana cream on one of the cookies. Garnish with a slice of banana and a dollop of whipped cream and sprinkle crushed vanilla wafer cookies on top, if desired. Repeat with the remaining cookies, and enjoy!

1 cup plus 2 tablespoons (135 g)
all-purpose flour

1 teaspoon baking powder

¼ teaspoon plus ⅛ teaspoon salt

¾ cup (149 g) granulated sugar

4 ounces (113 g) cream cheese,
at room temperature

4 tablespoons (57 g) unsalted
butter, at room temperature

1 large egg, at room temperature

1 large egg yolk, at room
temperature

1½ teaspoons vanilla extract

Powdered sugar, for dusting

Gooey Butter Cake Cookies

Gooey Butter Cake was invented by mistake in 1930s St. Louis when a baker who was preparing a standard cake batter mixed up the butter and flour proportions. The results were unexpectedly delicious: a sweet, dense, gooey cake that became an overnight success. Now you can enjoy this classic dessert in one chewy cookie. Dusted with powdered sugar and sprinkled with Southern hospitality, these gooey, buttery cookies will unmistakably capture your heart.

Make the Dough: In a small bowl, whisk together the flour, baking powder, and salt. Set aside.

In a large mixing bowl, beat the granulated sugar, cream cheese, and butter on medium speed until light and fluffy. Add the egg, egg yolk, and vanilla and beat until smooth. Then add the flour mixture and beat until no dry streaks remain. Cover the bowl with plastic and refrigerate for at least 2 hours. Dough can keep in the fridge for up to 1 week.

Bake the Cookies: Preheat the oven to 350°F (177°C) and line one or more baking sheets with parchment paper.

Scoop 1½ tablespoons dough into a ball and place it on the prepared baking sheet. Repeat with the remaining dough, leaving 2 inches of space between each one.

Bake for 8 to 10 minutes, until the edges are lightly golden and the centers no longer appear wet. If baking two pans at once, swap the positions of the pans halfway through to ensure the cookies bake evenly.

Let the cookies cool on the baking sheet for 5 minutes, then transfer to a wire rack to cool completely. Dust the cookies with powdered sugar before serving, and enjoy!

1¾ cups (210 g) all-purpose flour

1¼ cups (130 g) graham cracker crumbs (about 8 crackers)

1 teaspoon baking soda

1 teaspoon salt

2 sticks (226 g) unsalted butter, at room temperature

1 cup (213 g) brown sugar

½ cup (99 g) granulated sugar

2 large eggs, at room temperature

2 teaspoons vanilla extract

1½ cups (255 g) semisweet chocolate chips

3 to 4 milk chocolate bars, broken into pieces

7 to 8 graham crackers, broken into pieces

¾ to 1 cup mini marshmallows, cut in half (see note)

Note: If mini marshmallows are unavailable, simply cut larger marshmallows into ½-inch pieces.

Toasted Marshmallow S'mores Cookies

Invoke the spirit of summer with these campfire confections. In this easy recipe, graham cracker crumbs are infused into the dough with loads of chocolate chips. They're topped with graham cracker pieces, chunks of milk chocolate bars, and mini marshmallows, baked until toasty and golden. These cookies are made in the oven—no firewood required—so you won't have to wait until your next campout to enjoy your favorite summertime sweets.

Make the Dough: In a small bowl, whisk together the flour, graham cracker crumbs, baking soda, and salt. Set aside.

In a large mixing bowl, beat the butter, brown sugar, and granulated sugar on medium speed until light and fluffy. Add the eggs and vanilla and beat until smooth. Then add the flour mixture and beat until no dry streaks remain. Add the chocolate chips and beat until evenly distributed in the dough. Cover the bowl with plastic and refrigerate for at least 2 hours. Dough can keep in the fridge for up to 1 week.

Bake the Cookies: Preheat the oven to 350°F (177°C) and line one or more baking sheets with parchment paper.

Scoop 2 tablespoons dough into a ball and place it on the prepared baking sheet. Repeat with the remaining dough, leaving 3 inches of space between each one.

Bake for 8 minutes, then top each cookie with a few pieces of milk chocolate and graham crackers, pressing them gently into the half-baked cookies. Bake for an additional 3 to 5 minutes, until the edges are golden and the centers no longer appear wet. Remove the cookies from the oven and set the oven to broil.

Top each cookie with a few mini marshmallow halves, then place the baking sheet under the broiler until the marshmallows are toasted and browned, 1 to 3 minutes—be sure to

watch the cookies carefully so the marshmallows don't burn. If using two baking sheets, broil only one at a time.

Let the cookies cool on the baking sheet for 5 minutes, then transfer to a wire rack to cool completely. Enjoy!

2½ cups (300 g) all-purpose flour

1 teaspoon baking soda

½ teaspoon salt

1¼ cups (266 g) brown sugar

2 sticks (226 g) unsalted butter, at room temperature

1 large egg, at room temperature

2 teaspoons vanilla extract

36 to 38 (½-inch) chewy caramel candies (see note)

Flaky sea salt, for garnish

Note: For the caramel candies, any soft and chewy caramel will work, including chocolate-covered caramels like Rolos. The caramels should be no more than ½ inch long to avoid leakage during baking; if they are larger than that, use a knife to cut them down to ½ inch.

Salted Caramel Lava Cake Cookies

These crowd-pleasing volcanic treats are visually stunning and explode with flavor. Thankfully, they are simple to make. You just take your favorite caramel (like a Rolo), tuck it into the center of the dough, then bake, and that's it! The result is a soft and chewy brown sugar cookie with a molten caramel middle. Sprinkled with flaky sea salt, these lava cake–inspired cookies are dangerously delicious when eaten warm, and even better with a scoop of vanilla ice cream.

Make the Dough: In a small bowl, whisk together the flour, baking soda, and salt. Set aside.

In a large mixing bowl, beat the brown sugar and butter on medium speed until light and fluffy. Add the egg and vanilla and beat until smooth. Then add the flour mixture and beat until no dry streaks remain. Cover the bowl with plastic and refrigerate for at least 2 hours. Dough can keep in the fridge for up to 1 week.

Bake the Cookies: Preheat the oven to 350°F (177°C) and line one or more baking sheets with parchment paper.

Scoop 1½ tablespoons dough into a ball, then flatten it to a disc shape. Place one caramel candy in the center, then wrap the dough around the candy, sealing it inside the ball. Place the ball on the prepared baking sheet, then repeat with the remaining dough, leaving 2 inches of space between each one. Place the baking sheets in the freezer for 15 minutes; this helps keep the caramel inside the cookies while baking.

Transfer the baking sheets directly to the oven and bake for 12 to 14 minutes, until the edges of the cookies are lightly golden. If baking two pans at once, swap the positions of the pans halfway through to ensure the cookies bake evenly.

Let the cookies cool on the baking sheet for 5 minutes, then transfer to a wire rack to cool completely. Sprinkle each one with a pinch of sea salt, and enjoy!

Tiramisu Cloud Cookies

For the Cookies

1½ cups (180 g) all-purpose flour

2 teaspoons instant espresso powder

¾ teaspoon baking powder

¼ teaspoon salt

1 cup (113 g) powdered sugar

1 stick (113 g) unsalted butter, at room temperature

1 large egg, at room temperature

1 tablespoon Kahlua or other coffee liqueur, plus more for brushing

1 teaspoon vanilla extract

For the Mascarpone Cream

¾ cup (170 g) mascarpone cheese, at room temperature

3 tablespoons unsalted butter, at room temperature

1½ cups (170 g) powdered sugar

1½ teaspoons vanilla extract

¼ teaspoon salt

Unsweetened cocoa powder, for dusting

We couldn't finish this chapter without mashing up one of the most iconic Italian desserts. Tiramisu, which means "pick me up" or "cheer me up," is guaranteed to do just that—especially in the form of a light, airy cookie. When these soft, coffee-flavored cookies come out of the oven, they're brushed with Kahlua while still warm. Once cooled, they're topped with a smooth vanilla mascarpone cream and lightly dusted with cocoa. Pick one up and it'll pick you right back up too!

Make the Dough: In a small bowl, whisk together the flour, espresso powder, baking powder, and ¼ teaspoon salt. Set aside.

In a large mixing bowl, beat the 1 cup powdered sugar and 1 stick butter on medium speed until light and fluffy. Add the egg, Kahlua, and 1 teaspoon vanilla and beat until smooth. Then add the flour mixture and beat until no dry streaks remain. Cover the bowl with plastic and refrigerate for at least 2 hours. Dough can keep in the fridge for up to 1 week.

Bake the Cookies: Preheat the oven to 350°F (177°C) and line one or more baking sheets with parchment paper. Pour a few tablespoons of Kahlua into a small bowl or measuring cup and set aside.

Scoop 1½ tablespoons dough into a ball and place it on the prepared baking sheet. Repeat with the remaining dough, leaving 2 inches of space between each one.

Bake for 8 to 10 minutes, until the edges are lightly golden and the centers no longer appear wet. If baking two pans at once, swap the positions of the pans halfway through to ensure the cookies bake evenly. As soon as they come out of the oven, brush each cookie lightly with Kahlua.

Let the cookies cool on the baking sheet for 5 minutes, then transfer to a wire rack to cool completely.

Make the Mascarpone Cream: In a large mixing bowl, beat the mascarpone and 3 tablespoons butter on medium speed until light and fluffy. Sift in the 1½ cups powdered sugar to remove any lumps and beat until combined. Then add the 1½ teaspoons vanilla and ¼ teaspoon salt and beat until smooth.

Assemble the Cookies: Spread about 1 tablespoon mascarpone cream on each of the cookies in a smooth layer. Dust them lightly with cocoa powder, and enjoy!

conclusion

This is not the end. In fact, it's only the beginning. Cookies are love, and it's our goal to spread as much as we can. The more cookies we all share, the better this planet will be. You can start right now by surprising your neighbor with a gift bag filled with Dark Chocolate Peanut Butter Truffles (page 60), or showing your appreciation to your mail carrier by leaving them a basket of Gingerbread Crinkles (page 70), or presenting your coworkers with a plate of On-the-Go Blueberry Breakfast Bars (page 196) to start the morning off right. There are so many ways to inspire smiles in everyone—they're just waiting inside of each individual to light up the day. And what better way to bring that out of someone than with a fresh batch of homemade cookies?

Cookies are cosmic, perfect, little bite-size treats, and each one tells a story. Let this be the beginning of your cookie crusade. May you encounter countless cookie coincidences on your cookie quest. You will find a recipe for everyone in this book—you're about to make a lot of people very happy. Just don't forget to treat yourself, too, because when you smile, the world smiles with you, and That Takes the Cookie.

Happy Baking!
Ryan and Adam

acknowledgments

To our family and friends, for the continuous outpouring of love and support and for cheering us on from the beginning. Or was it all for the cookies?

To Leigh Eisenman, for reaching out to us in 2016, and for being the best literary agent, advisor extraordinaire, and occasional therapist we could ever ask for.

To Ronnie Alvarado, for believing in us and for inviting us to be a part of this sweet project. We are honored to be a part of the Simon Element family—thanks for making the entire process feel like a party!

To Rachel Saltzman, our superhero manager, who has been with us from day one. Your friendship over the years and business expertise have been invaluable.

To Lauren Volo, for your exceptional artistry and for making every photo look museum-worthy. It was such a treat watching you work your magic in your photography studio, and this book would not be the same without your creative touch. Thank you for making these photos look beyond anything we imagined.

To Mira Evnine, for your gorgeous styling, deep conversations, and killer music playlists. Your masterful decorating skills and mesmerizing shmears help make this book shine. We can't thank you enough.

To Megan Litt, for your baking wizardry and warm smiles. We still can't comprehend how you were able to whip up all these recipes so swiftly and smoothly in just seven days. Working with you was a dream, and we hope to do it again soon.

To Soli Zardosht, for jumping in for Megan one day. Thank you for bringing so much love to the photography studio, as well as your talented baking skills. It was so fun getting to know you.

To Maeve Sheridan at Hero & Beauty, for lending us your cute and colorful props.

To Emmett and Kitt Herceg, for allowing us to use your adorable hands in our photos, and for helping us eat all the cookies at the end of each photo shoot day.

To Heather Heels, for bringing rays of positive vibes and love every day to the studio.

To Ophelia (Lauren's dog), for sitting on our feet to show your affection, and for endless cuddles during the photo shoot.

To the Alpenglow Clan, for testing and tasting a few of our recipes, and for all your helpful feedback. Special shout-out to Holly for always keeping the kitchen floor spotless.

To the Calabasas Crew, for (most of) your clever puns and middle-of-the-night book title inspiration.

To Josh and Arlo, for being the most welcoming hosts and for always introducing us to great music. Thanks for your insightful input with this book and for helping taste all our treats.

To our friends Saunder Choi, Gloria Chamarro, Ellie Wyatt, Christina Xenos, and Alex Lyras, for helping us with foreign languages in the recipe headnotes in the Cookies 'Round the World chapter.

To the Goglia family, for including us in your epic annual Easter gala, and for taste-testing half of the A Bar Walks into a Cookie chapter. We appreciate your *feed*-back, and we look forward to crashing your party again next year. We'll bring the cookies.

To Ryan's choir, The L.A. Choral Lab, for devouring dozens of our cookies every week at rehearsal. Thank you for finishing off all our extra baked goods so we didn't have to eat them all.

To Rebecca Firth, the Cookie Queen, for your amazing

friendship and guidance over the years, delicious cocktails, and seriously legit homemade sourdough pizza.

To Aunt Carolyn, for your boundless love, easy laugh, and for inspiring our Dark Chocolate Peanut Butter Truffles (page 60). We know you would love them.

To Glenn Carlos, for sharing his Grandma Helen's recipe that inspired our Haunted Halloween Haystacks (page 138), and extra-special thanks for introducing the two of us in a recording studio in 2001.

To Ginny and Doug Erickson at Erickson Surfaces, for your friendship, creative artistry, and unwavering support.

To our oven that died in the middle of recipe testing—that really took the cookie!

To everyone who has supported us over the years on our blog and on social media, and has made our recipes at home. Thank you!

Corrections page—We thought it would be helpful to add a page on our website that will list any corrections or mistakes that may appear in this book. As meticulous and organized as we are, we are not perfect, so in case there are any errors, you will find a list of corrections at www.husbandsthatcook.com/whoops. There is a place to comment, so please let us know if you find any mistakes in these pages.

Website—Visit us at www.husbandsthatcook.com and sign up for our email list to stay up-to-date with more Husbands' recipes and all the latest news. Come say hello, and let us know if you have any questions or comments—we would love to hear from you!

Social media—We can't wait to see what you make from the book, so use the hashtag #ThatTakesTheCookie on social media so we can see your creations.

index